Introduction to Men's Gymnastics

DATE DUE		
11 =	8/31/07	
3 2		

Introduction to Men's Gymnastics

by Doug Alt with Alfred Glossbrenner

HAWTHORN BOOKS, INC.
Publishers/New York
A Howard & Wyndham Company

INTRODUCTION TO MEN'S GYMNASTICS

Library of Congress Catalog Card Number: 79-84327

ISBN: 0-8015-4081-X

1 2 3 4 5 6 7 8 9 10

Designed by Judith Neuman

Contents

Introduction to Men's Gymnastics

1
Gymnastics for Fun and Fitness

Gymnastics is like no other sport in the world. It's fun to watch and even more fun to take part in. It emphasizes strength and power, beauty and grace. It can be elegantly simple or enormously complex. And it both rewards originality and demands perfection. It is a sport with but one major goal: to display the marvelous things the human body is capable of when properly conditioned and trained. Indeed, in gymnastics, the body is everything. That's why it's often called the purest sport.

Not that the apparatus and equipment aren't important—they are. But their main function is really to provide a framework for showing off a wide range of gymnastics skills. Unlike other sports, the focus isn't on where a ball is on the field or on how far an object is thrown, hit, or kicked. In gymnastics, the focus is exclusively on the individual performer and the skills he displays.

The interesting thing is that almost all of these skills are derived from what are essentially basic human movements. Activities like running, jumping, climbing, and swinging, for instance, come naturally to all of us. But they are also the main building blocks of gymnastics. Of course these movements have been refined and are often raised to their highest form in the sport. But even in the most advanced gymnastics routines you can spot movements that even little children can do almost instinctively.

This is important because it means that right from the start, without ever having been formally introduced to the sport, you have probably

1

already had some "gymnastic" experience. You may not yet know how to do a double back somersault on the tumbling mats or an iron cross on the rings, but chances are you've got some idea of the kind of strength, agility, and control those things require. That makes it easy to appreciate gymnastics stunts and, more importantly, easy to imagine how much fun it would be to do them.

Actually, when you watch a gymnast perform, it's hard to avoid feeling that with the right kind of training you could be out there doing stunts and tricks too. And you could. After all, you've got the same basic body with the same muscles and bones. Everything else—the skill, the experience, the muscular development—can be acquired through training and "working the apparatus," as gymnasts say. So why not?

Recently a lot of people have been asking that question, and the phenomenal growth and popularity of gymnastics in this country over the past few years have been the result. In 1969, for example, close to 40,000 Americans were involved in gymnastics. By 1978, that figure had shot up to 500,000 and it's still growing.

I can remember going to high school in the late 1950s when there were only three schools teaching men's gymnastics teams in the entire state. Today there are about 4,500 high school teams nationwide. There are also nearly 200 colleges with teams, and many of them offer athletic scholarships to gymnasts of outstanding ability or potential. In addition, there are some 3,000 private gymnastics clubs in the country, with more being added every month.

The private clubs or gyms are particularly important, for they are not only the fastest growing part of the sport, but they are also the places that tend to produce the highest level of achievement. Often this is because clubs have more equipment and can offer much smaller classes than are possible elsewhere. And there's also the fact that a gymnast can usually spend more time practicing his routines at a private gym than would be possible at most other facilities.

Private gyms make it possible for gymnasts to start at an earlier age—sometimes as young as seven, eight, or nine—than it would if training were left to a high school physical education program. That's why it's becoming increasingly common for some young men to be state champions by the time they start their freshman year.

Early achievements like that are very impressive by American standards, but they wouldn't be all that surprising to most Europeans, for in Europe, gymnastics has traditionally been a key element of physical education. Gymnastics there is treated as the basis for all sports, and classes in it begin in elementary school. That will probably never happen here, where gymnastics is still considered as just one of a dozen or more subject areas to be taught in physical education. But thanks to the growing popularity of the sport, the United States is gradually beginning to catch up.

A Visual Art Form

There are many reasons why gymnastics is becoming so popular. The nation's increased awareness of the need for physical fitness is certainly an obvious one. But there's something else that all too many people overlook. And that's simply that gymnastics is *fun.*

If you've ever swung on a rope or a tree limb or gone off a diving board or even vaulted over a fence, you know what I mean. Those things are fun to do purely for their own sake. I don't know just why this is, but I feel that it has something to do with the human body itself and the way we're put together.

Our bodies weren't meant to lead sedentary lives. They were designed to run and jump and swing and generally be active. Maybe this is because up until only a short time ago we *had* to be active just to survive.

But whatever the reason, the fact is that when we are active, something deep inside us responds and we feel good—about ourselves and about our bodies. That's what makes gymnastics so much fun. And no matter how far you advance in the sport, the feeling never leaves you.

Of course man has always been a competitive creature, so it's only natural that once you can do something, you want to learn to do it really well. And in gymnastics, that leads to a higher level of enjoyment.

It's fun to learn a new trick and to move your body in a new way. But it's even more satisfying to master the trick so completely that you can do it perfectly. This can take some time. For instance, you can learn the basics of how to do double leg circles on the pommel horse in a few practice sessions, but it may take you several years to get the stunt down to perfection.

Your hard work, though, pays off in the end, not only in personal satisfaction but also in competition. As a sport, gymnastics puts a heavy emphasis on perfection. The difficulty of the stunts you perform is important, too. But in general, it's better to do an easier trick perfectly than to do a more difficult one imperfectly. (Since gymnastics competition is divided into several levels, you'll be competing only with people of your own age and experience.)

One of the main reasons perfection is so important is that gymnastics is a sport in which the competitor is a *performer*. Gymnastics is meant to be viewed by other people, and gymnasts perform movements with their bodies that are designed to be both pleasing and impressive to watch. In other words, gymnastics is really a visual art form like sculpture, painting, or photography. The difference is that instead of stone, paint, or film, the gymnast uses his body.

That means that the appearance of a stunt and of the gymnast as he performs it becomes very important. Gymnasts are always concerned with how a stunt looks or with the "aesthetics" of a certain movement, and with good reason. Aesthetics is a key principle in competitive gymnastics. It's why perfection is so prized. (A perfectly executed stunt simply *looks* better than one that is not.) And it's the basis of the scoring system used to judge a performer's routine.

A body arranged in straight lines, for example, is visually more pleasing than one that is all angles. So whenever possible, gymnasts keep their knees straight and their toes pointed during most of their stunts. This creates a straight line from hip to toe.

Aesthetics is also the reason why the most efficient movement—the one that uses the least amount of energy—is usually considered the most expert. In fact, one of the main differences between a beginner and a more advanced gymnast is that the beginner hasn't learned the most efficient way to do a stunt. Beginners often use a lot of unnecessary strength; later they learn all the little tricks of weight shifting and leverage that help them do a stunt without struggling. This is important because one of the goals in gymnastics is to make even the most difficult stunts look easy.

Challenging the Mind

The emphasis on appearances or aesthetics means that a gymnast must concentrate on the detailed coordination of his body. And that requires a mental discipline that's unlike anything else in sports. In a ball sport, for example, you've got to concentrate on throwing the ball to another player or on getting it through the hoop. That means you've got to think about the muscles involved in getting the ball off exactly the way you want it. But you don't have to concentrate at the same time on where your right leg is, whether your left toes are pointed, and so forth.

If a gymnast doesn't concentrate on those things, he loses points, for in gymnastics every part of your body must be controlled at every moment. As you can imagine, this requires a new way of thinking and—at the most advanced levels—a tremendous mental discipline. The need for complete concentration makes gymnastics a great experience mentally, and I think the things you learn from it probably carry over into other parts of life.

I know gymnastics can give your self-confidence a real boost, and that's important in everything you do. It can also be a help in showing you how to deal with fears and apprehensions, and it can teach you a lot about problem-solving.

For example, the first time you get up on the horizontal bar you may be a little scared. You'll be hanging from a bar that's more than eight feet off the floor and will be expected to swing around and do tricks while holding on with only your fingers. That's bound to be a little frightening.

But overcoming your fear won't be that hard, for long before you attempt a stunt at eight feet, you'll have practiced it with the bar at a much lower setting. And instead of viewing the stunt as a single large problem, you'll learn to attack it one step at a time, getting one piece of it under control before moving on to the next.

This philosophy of "divide and conquer" is so basic to gymnastics that it will become a habit. And since it's so effective in the gym, it won't be long before you find yourself applying it to other problems as well.

Enjoyment That Never Ends

It may take awhile to learn, but once you perform a stunt success-fully, the feeling of satisfaction you get is almost impossible to describe. It's an incredible personal high. You feel good about yourself. You're proud that you've shown you are the master of your body. And you're proud that you've accomplished something most people can't do.

The first time I felt that satisfaction was when I did my first pullover on the high bar without the coach's assistance. It was a great sensation, and I've experienced it many times since. In fact, the feeling can be a little addictive. Once you've conquered one stunt, you want to go back and do it a little better. And you want to find another stunt to master. Gymnasts are hooked on gymnastics precisely because of this, and as one stunt leads to another, things just keep building and building.

The marvelous thing is that the feeling never goes away. A gymnast can go for forty years, working out in the gym every day, and *still* find new challenges that are just as satisfying as learning to do his first back flip. That's what keeps him in there.

Body Building Made Easy

That feeling of accomplishment is certainly what attracted me to gymnastics, although I got into it in a roundabout way. When I was in junior high school I thought I was a pretty hot sandlot quarterback. So when I got to high school I naturally went out for the football team. At that point I was about four feet nine or four feet ten inches tall, and I weighed in at ninety-six pounds. Not quite a "ninety-seven-pound weakling," but almost. The football team didn't even have a workout uniform small enough to fit me.

So I went out for the gymnastics team instead. Between my sophomore and junior years I gained forty pounds and shot up to close to my present height of five feet ten inches. But by then I was hooked. I had found out how much fun gymnastics could be and never gave quarterbacking a second thought.

That's one of the beauties of gymnastics. It's an ideal sport for the person who's not big enough to play basketball or football. In fact, it actually favors a smaller person. A linebacker, for instance, has so much weight that he wouldn't be able to hold himself up on the parallel bars without having his arms give way. A tall person, say someone who's six feet two inches tall, is also at a major disadvantage. He's so tall that when he hangs on the rings or on the high bar his feet will touch the ground. He won't be able to swing through without bending his knees and ankles.

That's not to say that a tall person can't do gymnastics. We've had some outstanding tall gymnasts on the side horse, for example. And since their height gives them such long lines, they look very dramatic as they swing around with their legs outstretched. There have been some fantastic tall guys who have won generous scholarships to college and have gone on to become national champions in some events.

So you never know. In general, though, the ideal height for a gymnast is somewhere between five feet three and five feet seven inches tall, with a body weight between 125 and 145 pounds. I'd say that almost all world class gymnasts today are under 150 pounds.

Actually, weight is probably the main physical limitation. You simply cannot be a gymnast if you're overweight. That doesn't mean you can't start working out if you're overweight right now. It just means that you'll want to drop the excess pounds fairly soon. And you really will want to, for gymnastics provides a tremendous motivation.

As you go into the gym, you're faced with that excess weight every time you try to pull yourself up onto a piece of equipment. You don't have to struggle long before you're saying, "I'd better either lose some weight or gain some strength." Usually you've got to do both at the same time.

You can lose the weight by going on a diet, but the strength will probably take care of itself. Gymnastics is a superb body builder. It's much more interesting than lifting weights and often results in well-developed and well-proportioned bodies.

The reason is simple. A gymnast is constantly lifting and moving his own weight around the gym. If you weigh 100 pounds, every time you pull yourself up on the high bar, it's like lifting a 100-pound weight; with every handstand you support a 100-pound weight over your head. Most stunts require you to move your weight around and control it very carefully, and that calls for even more strength than just lifting a weight.

As a result, your body will develop almost automatically as you work the apparatus. You won't have to do many special exercises. It will all happen naturally, and you'll enjoy yourself at the same time.

I ought to say at this point that while there is really no high or low age limit in gymnastics, there are a few strength tricks that normally aren't taught to younger gymnasts. I'm thinking particularly of high stress stunts like an iron cross on the rings. This stunt requires the gymnast to support himself on the rings with his arms stretched out to either side. It exerts a tremendous pull on the areas where the muscles are inserted into the arms. Therefore coaches don't teach it to boys until they become teen-agers and are physically more mature.

From Persia to the Present

Men have been performing gymnastics of one sort or another for centuries. Archaeological records show that the ancient Persians, Chinese, and Egyptians were familiar with this kind of exercise and probably originated many of the stunts we do today, though at the time, pleasure and performing weren't uppermost in their minds. In those days, gymnastics was used primarily to train soldiers to conquer new territory and to defend the homeland from invaders.

Later gymnastics was done more for enjoyment. To the ancient Greeks, the ideal man was a well-rounded person with a "healthy mind in a healthy body." Gymnastics helped on both counts, and its popularity undoubtedly contributed to the founding of the Olympic Games.

With the arrival of the Romans, gymnastics once again became something used primarily for military purposes. To train cavalrymen, the Romans developed a wooden horse on which a soldier could practice his mounts, dismounts, and trick riding. This later evolved into the pommel horse we use today.

Medieval knights also used the wooden horse, while some foot soldiers were trained in creating human towers for use near a castle's walls during a siege. Gymnastics also had a lighter side in the Middle Ages, and no town fair, jousting tournament, or court was complete without a troupe of tumblers and acrobats.

The eighteenth century saw the dawn of the Age of Reason or Enlightenment, a period which fancied itself the modern equivalent of the Golden Age of Greece. Gymnastics and an increased interest in the human body and physical training logically followed.

That interest grew. And by the nineteenth century it led to the creation of various "systems" of gymnastics in Germany, Switzerland, Sweden, and Denmark. When people from these countries emigrated to the United States, they brought their systems and love of gymnastics with them. German emigrants established American branches of their *Turnverein,* or turner clubs. The Swiss brought their Swiss Societies. And people from Czechoslovakia established *Sokol* units. All of these organizations helped establish gymnastics as a competitive sport in the United States, and some still exist today. The Y.M.C.A. and the Amateur Athletic Union (A.A.U.) also helped popularize gymnastics in this country.

When the Olympic Games were revived in 1896, they included a gymnastics event. As interest in the sport grew, so did the number of tournaments and international competitions.

Historically, though, the United States has not done very well in international gymnastics. The sport has traditionally been dominated by countries that place much more emphasis on gymnastics than we do. In some countries, for example, gymnastics is virtually a national sport, attracting more participants than almost all others. And for some countries international competition is a political arena where a victory is thought to be so important that competitors are encouraged, trained, and sometimes supported by the state so that they may perfect their skills. This, combined with the fact that until relatively recently the United States didn't use all of the same events as the rest of the world in its domestic competition, has been at least partially responsible for our lack of success.

There are indications, however, that all that is changing. The growing American interest in gymnastics is having a definite effect. In November of 1978 at the World Championships in Strasbourg, France, the U.S. men's team placed fourth, and Kurt Thomas placed first in the world in floor exercise. Kurt was awarded a gold medal for his outstanding performance, the first gold medal won by a male U.S. gymnast in world competition in forty years!

Those of us close to the sport feel this is only the beginning. As more and more young men enter gymnastics, and as its popularity continues to spread, future champions are bound to emerge. More than ever before, it's a great time to become a gymnast.

2
Starting Out

Perhaps because of the warm climate or possibly as a holdover from their primitive past, the ancient Greeks customarily exercised in the nude. In fact the term *gymnastics* itself comes from the Greek word for nude (*gymnos*) and literally means "naked art." The world has come a long way since the seventh century B.C., and gymnastics has changed a great deal. But while birthday suits are no longer in fashion, you still don't need a lot of special equipment to do gymnastics.

Your Personal Equipment

A pair of shorts, a tee shirt, and a pair of athletic socks are about all you need to get started. Your shorts should be comfortable and non-binding. They should allow you full freedom of movement and shouldn't restrain your legs in any way. A pair of athletic or gym shorts or even a bathing suit will work very well. You should also wear an athletic supporter or a pair of the close-fitting, athletic-style undershorts that have come on the market in recent years.

Your tee shirt should give you maximum flexibility and freedom of movement, particularly in the chest, shoulders, and upper arms. Because of this, many gymnasts prefer sleeveless tee shirts, but really, any tee shirt is fine as long as it gives you plenty of room. If you're going to buy a tee shirt, remember that most are made of cotton and cotton tends to shrink in the wash. So be sure to get one that will still fit you when it comes out of the dryer.

Athletic socks are perfectly adequate footwear, but later, when you are more advanced or want to look especially good, you may decide to trade in your sweat socks for a pair of gymnastics slippers. Made of soft leather, cloth, or stretch fabric, gymnasts' slippers fit snugly over your feet and are held in place by an elastic band running across the top of the foot. The bottoms of the slippers have a thin rubber coating for improved traction on floor mats and apparatus.

When you become more advanced and begin to compete, you may also want to have a uniform. Gymnastics trousers are tapered to make sure the outline of the leg is visible, since this enhances the aesthetic effect of the performance. The pant legs end in stirrups that run across the bottoms of the feet and keep the trousers from riding up.

The uniform top looks like a sleeveless tee shirt, except that, like the trousers, it is often made of a stretch fabric. Usually the shirt is long enough to be tucked into the trousers and fastened under the crotch. This prevents it from being pulled out during a performance. Normally the pants are held up by suspenders, but one-piece "jump suit"-style uniforms are available in which top and bottom are sewn together.

If you can't find gymnastics slippers or competition uniforms at your local sporting goods store, you may have to order them through the mail. *International Gymnast,* the sport's primary magazine, frequently carries ads for companies that specialize in gymnastics gear. The magazine is located at 410 Broadway, Santa Monica, CA 90406, telephone (213) 451-4211. Your instructor may also be able to direct you to an appropriate manufacturer.

Although a sweat shirt and a pair of sweat pants aren't strictly necessary, they're definitely a good idea. They can be helpful not only for warming up your muscles but also for protecting your skin when you're learning certain skills. There are some stunts, for example, in which you hang on the parallel bars by your upper arms, or slide along the bar, or straddle the bars with your legs. If your skin is unprotected while you're learning these stunts, you may end up with a friction burn before you've mastered the technique. A sweat suit can make things a lot easier.

Protecting the skin on your hands is also essential. Basic and beginning stunts usually don't put much stress on your hands. But as you advance to more difficult skills and as you practice harder, your hands can become sore and hot. Of course, eventually the skin on your palms and fingers will get harder and become more resistant to stress. But even experienced gymnasts frequently wear handguards to protect their palms.

Handguards or grips are usually made of leather or a cotton lampwick material. They are designed to fit over the middle and ring fingers and run across the palm and up around the wrist where they are tied or buckled in place. They come in different sizes and thicknesses, and since each event affects a grip differently, advanced gymnasts may have a set of guards for each one.

Chalk can be very helpful, too. In fact, it's essential for most work on the apparatus. Gymnasts dust their hands with chalk (powdered magnesium carbonate) because it absorbs perspiration and gives them a better grip. Without chalk, your hands can become so wet with perspiration that you'll have trouble holding on and may even slip at a crucial moment.

Unfortunately, chalk can be a bit messy. (One of the reasons why gymnasts' trousers have traditionally been white is to prevent chalk smudges from showing.) So to save on cleanup work, some high schools don't provide it. However, chalk is available in block form from many drugstores and in powdered form from gymnastic equipment houses. If you're in a program that doesn't provide chalk, you might see if you can get permission to use your own personal supply. (For more information on how to care for your hands, please see the special section on the subject in chapter 6.)

The Apparatus—an Overview

The term "apparatus" is used to refer to all gymnastics equipment collectively and to each unit individually. (For pictures of each apparatus, please see the appropriate chapter.) Although basically simple in construction, most apparatus are the result of years and sometimes centuries of evolution and refinement. As a result, each piece of equipment used today is designed in the way that experience has shown is best suited to displaying particular gymnastics skills.

The apparatus include the pommel horse or side horse, the still rings, the long horse, the parallel bars, and the horizontal or high bar. The general skills that are to be performed on each of these pieces are spelled out right in the official rules of the sport. The side horse, for example, is to be used for "clean swings without stops." That usually means that the gymnast must support his body with straight arms on the horse while he circles his legs to the front and back, releasing his grip when necessary to allow his legs to pass.

Movements on the rings are supposed to alternate between swings, strength parts, and hold (balance) parts. Swinging, flight, and hold parts are the main qualities of stunts on the parallel bars. Flight, with the help of a springboard (a specially bent piece of wood with rubber treads over the takeoff area) is the essence of the long horse vault. And horizontal bar exercises must consist "exclusively of swinging parts without stops."

So as you can see, each piece of apparatus demands different skills. And, while it may be possible to compete in only one or two events at the high school and college levels, in the Olympics and other international contests a gymnast must be proficient enough to compete in *all* events. As more and more gymnastics competitions follow the nationwide trend toward the all-around format, gymnastics will become even more challenging for the gymnast and more exciting for the spectator.

Finding a Gym and Choosing a Program

Obviously gymnastics equipment is far too expensive for any one individual to buy. And gymnastics itself is not something you can learn completely on your own. So for reasons of safety, proper instruction, and equipment, you'll want to locate a gym and enroll in a gymnastics program with a qualified instructor.

For some people, a high school or college program satisfies these requirements. But unfortunately, many school programs can't offer the caliber of instruction, the supervision, and the practice time most gymnasts need. A private club, gym, or other establishment is often the answer.

A good first step in finding a gym and a gymnastics program is to check the yellow pages of your phone book. Look under "Gymnasiums," "Gymnastics Instruction," and "Health Clubs." You might also check with your Y.M.C.A., Y.M.H.A., or similar service organizations. In some cities, town recreation facilities are equipped for gymnastics practice and instruction. And, of course, there are the

Sokol groups and *Turnverein* (also spelled "Turn Verein") and Turner Societies mentioned in chapter 1.

Unless you live in some out-of-the-way place, putting together a list of gymnasiums and gymnastics programs shouldn't be too hard. However, choosing the one you want to enroll in calls for a bit more work. If possible, you should visit all of the places on your list. But if it's a long list, you may want to pare it down first by eliminating those places that aren't conveniently located. In any case, you should definitely try to visit a gym before you decide to enroll in its program.

Call them up and find out when they hold the level of class you'd like to join or when their team (if they have one) practices. Then make arrangements to go and watch. Take a look at the facilities. Is the apparatus well maintained? Are there plenty of safety mats? Do they have enough equipment for everyone in the class to get a good workout?

It's also an excellent idea to talk to the instructor who will be teaching your class. If you're a beginner, it's very important that the instructor be truly interested in teaching beginners. Some instructors are really most interested in coaching their teams and teach classes only as a sort of sideline. And that's not good because it probably means you'll get less attention than you need.

Of course this is not the kind of thing you can ask directly. But you can ask what the instructor does overall—how many beginner, intermediate, and advanced classes he teaches and whether he is also a coach of a team. Often you can tell where his interests lie by his response. If he's relatively unenthusiastic about the subject of classes but is off and running as soon as you ask about his team, it may be a clue that he's not the right instructor for you.

On the other hand, there are many excellent coaches who are also very fine instructors. I don't mean to imply that a man must be either one or the other. It's just that the relationship between instructor and student is so important, particularly for a beginner, that it's critical to find someone who is sincerely interested in teaching right from the start.

That's why it's a good idea to look for teaching experience in the background of any prospective instructor. A degree in physical education, for example. If a person doesn't have a phys. ed. degree, he should have a background in some other area of education with experience as a competitor on the college level.

In other words, what you're looking for is an educator. You're not looking for an Olympic star (who may be a great performer but not necessarily a good teacher), and at this stage you're not looking for a coach famous for his top teams. You need someone who can deal with you as a beginner and is interested in teaching you how to be an accomplished gymnast.

A prospective instructor should be more than happy to give you his background. If he refuses . . . well, maybe you should look someplace else.

Class Size and Cost

There really is no set optimum class size in gymnastics. Far more important is how much learning any one person does during the time he's in the gym. Obviously, learning can be maximized by a low teacher-to-student ratio. But even more important than that is the way a teacher works with each student.

This is a key point to watch for when you're observing a class at a prospective gym. Look to see how much activity any one person gets in a single fifteen-minute time span. If you see people standing in big lines or sitting down in line or waiting a long time to get on the apparatus, then there's a problem.

But the problem may not be with the size of the group. It may be more a question of management. A good teacher may be able to instruct a class of fifteen to twenty more effectively than another person could handle ten or twelve. For example, by setting up teaching stations around the gym and having students practice certain safe stunts at each station, a teacher can make sure the entire class gets a good workout and learns a lot at the same time.

Good class management can be important not only because it increases the speed with which you learn, but also because it avoids wasted time. And in gymnastics, wasted time can also mean wasted money. Not a lot of money. But because of the nature of the sport, it is often necessary to pay a certain amount for classes or for the use of a gym.

Gymnastics classes can cost anywhere from a few dollars to as much as $150 a month, depending upon the number of classes and where you enroll. Service organizations and town recreation facilities may be free, or they may charge a small fee, often less than $5 a month. Private gymnastics clubs and organizations involved in the business of teaching the sport usually charge by the class. The cost ranges from $2 to $2.50 per class up to as high as $7 or $8 a class, with many falling in the $5 to $6 per class range. What you usually get for a higher fee is a smaller class, closer supervision, the use of more specialized equipment, more mats, etc.

Naturally your total cost per month will also depend upon the number of classes you take each week. For a beginner, one or two classes a week is usually about right. Each class may be an hour, an hour and a half, or possibly two hours, depending upon how the program is organized.

Taking a class once or twice a week will get you into the sport and keep you learning. If you find that you enjoy gymnastics and like to do it for recreation, you can continue at that level for many, many years to come. For the last one hundred fifty years or so in Europe, many men have made a habit of going to the gym a couple of times a week until they're in their fifties or sixties. I myself have worked out with men sixty and seventy years old who have been into gymnastics all their lives. They still go to the gym and do some giant swings on the high bar and some work on the horse because they just enjoy the activity and like to stay limber and in condition.

Of course, if you're interested in joining a team and competing, you'll want to be in the gym more than twice a week. But for most people who are just starting out, one or two classes a week are fine.

A Typical Class

Different instructors have different ways of organizing their classes. But usually a class will run about an hour. During that time each student gets instruction on two or three pieces of apparatus. Usually that means spending twenty minutes to half an hour on each piece of equipment. This is something to keep in mind as you read this book. For the sake of clarity, the apparatus and skills for each competitive event have been presented as separate chapters. But that doesn't mean you must master all of the stunts in each chapter before moving on to the next. In class you'll be learning some skills for each event simultaneously.

Class sizes vary, but at a private club or gymnastics school, six to ten students per class is about average. At recreation centers and service organizations, classes will probably be somewhat larger.

Often an instructor will teach one or two students at a time on a particular piece of apparatus. While waiting for their turns with the instructor, the other students will be using the other apparatus to do strength work or to practice stunts that do not require the attention of the instructor. If the class is well managed, you'll be working almost all of the time, either learning new skills with the instructor or perfecting skills taught in previous classes.

Your instructor will probably also give you some exercises to do at home on days when you're not in class. These exercises will keep you limber, and, particularly in the case of a new gymnast, may be designed to build muscular strength and endurance. Strength is extremely important in gymnastics, and building and maintaining it is a never-ending battle. To build up your muscles and to keep them in top shape, you've got to do strength exercises at least three times a week. Otherwise your strength will quickly drop back down to its pre-exercise level. That's just the way the human body works—if you don't use it, you lose it. So if you go to the gym once or twice a week, you've got to do some kind of exercise between each visit.

Your instructor will know best which exercises (push-ups, sit-ups, etc.) and how many repetitions of each exercise you personally should do. And you almost certainly won't need any equipment. However, one of those inexpensive chinning bars that fits in a doorway might come in handy.

Playing it Safe

After seeing a performer do a double back somersault dismount from the high bar or some other impressive stunt, it's not unusual for prospective gymnasts to ask, "Is gymnastics safe?" The answer is, yes, gymnastics is safe—if it is properly supervised, if the proper equipment is used, and if the gymnast learns his skills in the proper progression.

Proper supervision includes the use of "spotting" on difficult stunts. The "spotter" places himself in a position where he can reach out to prevent a performer from falling—or if that isn't possible, to catch or deflect and cushion the performer's fall. Spotting is also useful in teaching a stunt, since the spotter can reach out and help the performer move his body in the correct way, as during a handstand or a flip.

Safety belts, mats, and crash pads are important pieces of equipment that should be used in all gyms. The safety belt is a leather or
fabric belt with a rope attached to a swivel on each side. The belt fits
around the waist, and the ropes are run through pulleys attached to
ceiling beams and then down to the floor. By holding on to the rope, the
instructor or spotter can keep a gymnast from falling while he's learning
a new stunt on the high bar or rings or other apparatus. Usually,
though, a safety belt isn't needed until the gymnast progresses to
advanced stunts.

Mats, on the other hand, are used from the very first day. In the past,
gym mats were made of hair or fiber and covered with canvas. But in
recent years these materials have been replaced by plastic-covered
foam pads of various thicknesses and densities. The standard tumbling
mat, for example, is usually one to two inches thick. It's relatively firm
and is designed not only to absorb the shock of cartwheels, forward
rolls, and other tumbling stunts, but also to provide some bounce or lift
when you hit it hard enough. This resilience is particularly important
when, at more advanced levels, you begin running to do flips in the air.

The competition landing mat is about four inches thick. If you cut it
open, you'd find that it consists of two layers of foam. One layer is about
the same thickness and firmness of the standard tumbling mat. The
other layer consists of two or more inches of softer foam. This mat can
be used in two ways: soft side up (when learning a tumbling stunt) or
firm side up (when learning or performing a dismount from the
apparatus).

There is also an eight-inch mat made completely of soft foam. This
mat should never be used alone. Eight inches of foam may sound like a
lot, but if you land on it from any significant height (as when doing a
dismount), it will quickly compress down to whatever's beneath it.
That's why you have to use it on top of at least one competition landing
mat and preferably two, or else use it with another eight-inch mat.

You may also be using a twelve-inch mat consisting of a one- or two-
inch layer of standard tumbling mat foam and a layer of ten to eleven
inches of soft foam. This mat can be used by itself with either the firm or
soft side up, depending upon the stunt you're doing. There are even
mats that are eighteen, twenty-four, and thirty-six inches thick. These
are similar to the crash pads you may have seen in high jump or pole
vault landing pits at track meets. Some gyms have four- to five-foot-
deep pits filled with foam or foam scraps for the same reason.

The quantity and variety of mats used are some of the things you should pay particular attention to when you're looking for a gym. If a gym doesn't have plenty of mats, it may be a signal that it doesn't emphasize safety as much as it should. But no matter how many mats a place has, none of them can help you if positioned improperly. So before you get on the apparatus, it's a good idea to always make sure that the mats are where they're supposed to be.

Learning things in the correct sequence is the third main safety requirement. As in most sports, a large portion of gymnastics injuries occurs when a person tries something before he knows how to go about it. When you see someone else do some spectacular stunt, it's perfectly understandable to want to try the same thing yourself. But unless you're properly prepared, it's also a good way to hurt yourself. In gymnastics, one skill is built upon another, and if you try some new trick before you've mastered the skills leading up to it, you're just asking for trouble.

Finally, you should also play it safe by warming up before you start your workout. If you don't, you won't be able to do your best work. And there's a good chance you'll pull a muscle.

Your instructor will tell you which exercises to do. Most beginners need only some basic stretching exercises. But as you advance and begin doing more difficult stunts, you'll need other exercises. You'll have to stretch and warm up differently for each piece of apparatus. If you're going to work on the pommel horse, for example, you may not do an Achilles tendon stretch (the Achilles tendon joins the muscles in the calf of the leg to the bone of the heel), but if you're going to work on your tumbling and floor exercise, you would definitely do it. Even in competition, when a performer is on deck, you'll probably find him doing his warm-ups. It just doesn't make sense to neglect them.

3
Tumbling

Tumbling is the foundation of gymnastics. Long before there was any apparatus, or even nice soft mats, men were practicing and perfecting the same basic skills we use today. And over the centuries just about every possible way of moving the body has been explored.

Tumbling shows you how to manipulate and move your arms, legs, head, and entire body. It teaches your muscles what to do to achieve a particular effect, and it generally gives you a feel for gymnastics.

Later, the same basic moves you learn on the tumbling mat will be transferred to the apparatus. Indeed it's often been said that gymnastics as a whole is essentially tumbling performed on various pieces of equipment. That's an oversimplification, of course, but there's a lot of truth in it.

The best way to learn any tumbling stunt is to take it in small steps. I can't stress this enough. Gymnastics skills build upon one another, so it's essential to follow the steps involved in mastering a trick in the exact order in which the steps are presented. By doing this you'll learn each stunt safely and avoid developing bad habits that may be difficult to correct later on.

Tumbling as an Event

Tumbling used to be a regular event in competitive gymnastics, but now it has been largely replaced by floor exercise. As we'll see in the next chapter, floor exercise requires splits, flexibility stunts, and balancing in stationary positions. Tumbling skills are linked together with these feats into a smooth routine.

Yet tumbling competition is by no means dead. Today it's an important event in a relatively new activity called Acrosport. In addition to tumbling, Acrosport includes trampoline competition and balancing events in which two or more performers are involved in things like building human pyramids or doing hand balances on each other.

At an Acrosport event, tumbling competitions take place on seventy-five- to eighty-foot long mats with fifteen additional feet added as a runway. Performers begin at one end and use stunts like handsprings and cartwheels to travel the length of the mat. The rules vary from one organization to another, but they usually call for two or three runs down the mat. On one pass you may be required to do a lot of nontwisting somersaults, while on your second pass you may be expected to emphasize twisting as well. The scores for all of your passes are usually added together.

You get a rest between runs, of course, but the event still requires a lot of strength, power, and endurance; certainly more than floor exercise. Competitive tumbling may also be a bit more exciting, for it's hard to beat the dramatic impact of a high-speed, eighty-foot long tumbling routine packed with as many high difficulty stunts as possible.

In the near future it will probably become more exciting still, thanks to the new spring tumbling runways. These are six-foot-wide platforms that are eighty feet long and about a foot deep. The platform consists of hundreds of wooden strips that look like skis with the bowed part facing up or hundreds of small metal springs covered with a wooden surface. The platform or surface is covered with a long tumbling mat. The result is a tumbling surface with a lot of spring and lift to it.

Tumblers are already doing some phenomenal tricks on these spring runways. Some gymnasts are doing triple back tucked somersaults or double somersaults in absolutely straight body position. No tuck. No pike. Just end over end.

So even though it's no longer an official part of gymnastics, tumbling is very much alive and kicking. In fact, many full-fledged gymnasts also compete in tumbling and other Acrosport events.

The Lunge and the Tuck

The lunge and the tuck will be used in many tumbling stunts, so it's important to learn them right at the start.

The lunge, a basic starting position for many stunts

The lunge is a basic starting position used for getting into various stunts. In spite of its name, it's really a static position. To take a lunge position, stand with your arms up over your head. Put one leg out in front of you about two feet and bend that leg at the knee. Lean forward, but keep your rear leg straight. This will mean you'll want to come up onto the ball of your rear leg foot. That's all there is to it.

You'll be using this position to get into handstands, cartwheels, handsprings, and lots of other stunts.

To learn the tuck position, lie on your back and draw your legs up so your knees and thighs are against your chest and stomach. Your chin should be tucked down onto your chest, and your heels should be held in as near to your seat as possible. Next, put your hands on your knees and rock forward and backward very gently. Try to rock enough so that your head touches the mat as you go back and your heels just about touch the mat as you go forward.

Do this several times until you get used to the way it feels. Then take your hands off your knees and try to hold the same position with muscle power. Put your hands back by your ears, palms facing the mat, fingers close to your ears. Then rock back gently until your hands touch the mat and go forward as before.

Keep doing this until you become familiar with the way it feels. Then work on building up a little speed. Eventually you should rock fast enough to be able to roll forward and up onto your feet so that you're in a squat stand, with your hands in the same side-of-the-head position.

You've just learned the tuck position and the second half of the forward roll. Now let's learn the first half and put it all together into a complete stunt.

Single Forward Roll

The forward roll is one of the most basic and important stunts in tumbling. It's used in almost all floor exercise routines of all levels and can be performed either as a lead-in to another stunt or as part of a series of forward rolls.

The ultimate goal is to begin from a standing position, bend down, tuck your head, and roll forward quickly enough to end up standing on your feet in a squat tuck position. You've already learned the second part. Here's how to do the first.

THE FORWARD ROLL

a. Inch your toes forward. . .

b. as you tuck your head. . .

c. and roll over. . .

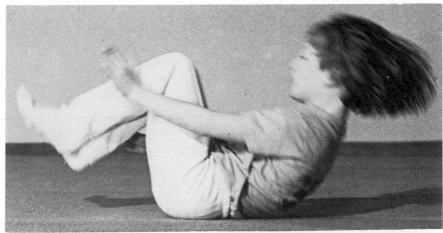

d. onto your back in a *tuck position*.

e. With a little speed, you'll come up out of the tuck. . .

f. and onto your feet.

As always, it's best to begin with a simple movement and gradually ease into the more difficult parts of the maneuver. So first, get down on all sixes (toes, knees, and hands) and practice bending your arms and touching your forehead to the mat in front of you.

Then come up to all fours (toes and hands) and practice bending your arms and neck so that the top of your head touches the mat. When you've done that a few times, inch your toes a bit closer to your hands and try to bend your arm and neck even more, so that the back of your head touches the mat. After trying this a couple of times, do it once again and hold the position. Then walk your toes even closer to your hands until you roll forward and over onto your back. Don't push yourself. Just inch your toes forward and let gravity do all the work.

Once you've got the feel of rolling over, you can try to add a little speed with the idea of building up enough momentum to carry you on through the roll and up onto your feet. The key to a roll like this is to tuck your body into as small a ball as possible and to get the back of your head onto the mat. If you place the top of your head on the mat, you're liable to get stuck in a headstand as you try to roll. Your knees and hips should be bent, and your chin should be tucked down onto your chest so that you're looking at your stomach.

To give yourself a little added speed, you can push off with your toes. This will take some trial and error, but eventually you will be able to roll forward and onto your feet in a squat tuck position.

If you aren't able to make it to your feet at this point, it's okay to use your hands to help push your body up. However, you should really try to do it without using your hands as soon as possible. This is both because it's better form and because the forward roll will eventually lead to other stunts in your floor exercise routine, and using your hands will interfere with the transition.

Now you're ready to try the entire stunt. Begin from a standing position with your hands at your sides. Squat down and put your hands about two feet in front of you. Bend your elbows and roll forward quickly enough to come up onto your feet. Then straighten up so that you're standing the same way you were at the start. With practice, you'll be able to make the entire stunt from beginning to end seem almost like a single smooth motion.

You should probably practice your tuck position with knees apart at first. This isn't good gymnastics form, but it prevents you from accidently hitting your mouth with your knees. In fact, whenever you're learning a rolling or tucking movement, it's a good idea to begin with knees apart. Later, when you've got it mastered, you can bring your knees together into the correct gymnastic form.

If after several attempts you find that your roll isn't smooth or that you're still landing on your back, you may need a little help from someone else. Your instructor or his assistant can help you tuck properly by putting his hand on the back of your neck and/or by helping you move your legs into a tighter, rounder tuck position.

Log Roll

This is a simple stunt that, even though it looks easy, is more challenging than you might imagine. You begin the log roll by lying across the mat on your stomach. Your legs should be together and straight, and your arms should be extended over your head. Try to keep your upper arms close to your ears, and your fingers together and pointed. Now all you do is roll down the mat a ways, stop, and roll back.

Once you've tried this a couple of times, do it again, only this time try to roll in a straight line. This isn't as easy as it sounds. But while it would be possible to suggest doing certain things to keep the roll straight, it's really best if you experiment and try to discover a technique for yourself.

This stunt is not used in floor exercise routines. But it's important because it teaches you a lot about how the body twists. You'll learn how to twist your body to either side, a vital skill in many other gymnastics stunts.

Tucked Head Balance

To perform this stunt, you begin in the same position used for learning the forward roll—that is, a squat with feet apart at shoulder width and hands eighteen to twenty-four inches apart on the mat in front of you. Lower your head to the mat so that it touches six inches to a foot beyond your hands. Your head should touch the mat at a point somewhere between these two extremes, perhaps just slightly above the hairline. You shouldn't be on your forehead and you shouldn't be on the top of your head.

Your head and two hands will thus form a triangle, which according to science is the most stable way to support anything. What *you're* going to support is the rest of your body. To do this, slowly inch your toes toward your hands until you can place one of your bent knees against the upper portion of one of your arms. Then slowly raise the toes of that leg from the mat. When you've done that, repeat the process with your other leg.

You may not be able to do it the first time. But you'll soon learn how to shift your weight so that you are in a balanced position with both feet off the mat. Hold that balance a moment or two, and then lower your toes to the mat and ease back into a squat.

Doing a tucked head balance is an achievement in itself. But later you'll use the same technique to perform a regular headstand. A similar technique will also be used for doing a shoulder stand on the parallel bars.

The tucked head balance

Jump with a Half Twist

Your goal here is to begin from a position similar to that used by swimmers doing a racing dive and then to shoot your arms over your head as you jump up into the air, and to do a half twist (either to the right or to the left). You should land on your feet facing the opposite direction and finish by lowering your arms to your sides.

Start by standing on the mat, knees bent and arms pointed out behind you. Your body should be bent forward slightly in a kind of half crouch. Swing your arms forward and upward until they are straight overhead with the upper arms in close to your ears. At the same time that you're swinging your arms, jump straight up and do a half twist in the air.

Don't jump really high at first. Try to jump only about an inch off the mat or so. That way you'll have less distance to fall if you should tip over to one side or another while in flight. Not all of your upward thrust has to come from your legs. Your arm swing can and should be used to increase your upward momentum, and it's well worth practicing since it is a central part of many advanced stunts.

As soon as you have done several one-inch jumps and successfully landed with your body under control, you can try for more height. There is no set optimum height for this stunt, but you should try for an inch or two more on each jump until you are able to point your toes while in the air. In fact, after you have the basic moves down, you should immediately begin working on your form. In this stunt that means keeping your knees straight, your legs together, and your toes pointed while you're in the air. This will create the kind of straight, pleasing line that judges look for in competition.

Although your knees should be straight while you're twisting, be sure to bend them slightly when you land. You should also bend a little at the waist as you come down. This will help absorb the shock. Then, after you're stable, rise to a standing position.

Be sure to learn how to do a twist in both directions. After you've mastered the stunt turning one way, work on turning in the opposite direction. You should eventually be able to do a jump with a half twist to the right or to the left equally well.

In doing this stunt, you want to try to land in exactly the same spot that you began from. That is, you don't want to travel to the left or right of your starting position as you twist. This may not be possible at first, but with practice you'll discover how to eliminate or control those movements that throw you off course.

a. Begin like a swimmer ready to do a racing dive.

JUMP WITH A HALF TWIST

b. Shoot your arms overhead as you jump and. . .

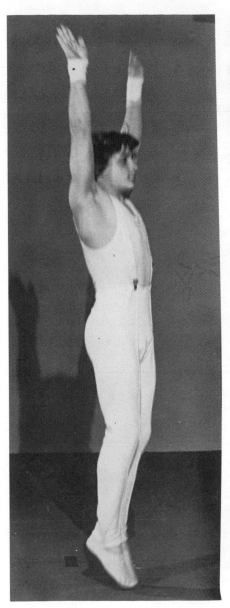

c. twist, toes pointed.   d. Land facing the opposite direction.

Jump with a Full Twist

This is basically the same stunt you just learned, except that you finish facing the same direction you faced at the start. The best way to master this stunt is to first master the half twist. Then try to twist a little more each time you jump. If you've learned the half twist correctly, getting enough height should be no problem. All you really have to do is learn to twist more quickly while you're in the air.

Three Forward Rolls

As soon as you try this stunt you'll see why it was so important to learn how to do a forward roll without using your hands to push yourself up to a stand at the finish. The stunt begins and ends just as a single forward roll did, but in between you do three rolls instead of one. This means that as soon as you've finished one roll you've got to plant your hands in front of you to begin another one, something you couldn't do if your hands were busy pushing your body up to the squat position at the end of the first roll.

You begin this stunt by executing a forward roll just as before, only instead of rising to a stand as you come out of it, you immediately do a second and then a third roll. The three rolls should flow together almost as if they were one long, continuous motion. As you come out of the third roll, you raise your arms straight over your head, holding them close to your ears, and stand up straight. As soon as you're on your feet and standing stable, you lower your arms to your sides to complete the trick.

Actually, even though it involves the same basic motion, this stunt is really three tricks. By doing it you learn how to start a roll from a stable position, how to keep a roll going, and how to stop a roll and then return to a stable position. These are skills that will be useful for cartwheels, handsprings, and other tumbling stunts, as well as for forward rolls.

Three Backward Rolls

A backward roll is somewhat more difficult than the forward roll, but it isn't really much harder to master—provided you use the right tumbling techniques. Begin by lying on your back in a tuck position.

a. Make yourself as round as possible in the squat position.

b. Sit back and roll like a ball.

c. Your feet come up over your head. . .

d. as you push up with your arms and slide your head out.

e. Bring your legs down on the other side. . .

f. landing on the balls of your feet. To prepare for the next backward roll, you would push off with your hands and bring them up near your ears (the "ready position").

Rock back and forth on your back, gradually building up speed. Then, instead of trying to rock up and onto your feet as you did in learning the forward roll, try to go the other way. See if you can rock backward and pull your feet over your head. Using your hands for support, try to balance yourself in this "almost over" position for a moment. Then rock back down again. Be sure to keep your knees bent and, while you're learning the stunt, keep them apart as well.

Next, rock back a little faster and try to get your toes and/or knees to touch the mat on the other side. Then push up with your arms and slide your head out. You should find yourself on hands and knees.

After you've done this once, try to land on the balls of your feet without allowing your knees to touch the mat. You may have to rock faster to do this, and you'll have to push off more with your arms. Your goal is to arrive in a squat position, resting on just the balls of your feet and your hands. When you've got that down, simply bring your hands up beside your ears. You're now in the "ready position" for the next roll.

Now try the trick starting from this squat position. Make yourself as round as you can while still keeping your balance. Then simply sit back and roll like a ball into the rest of the stunt. Be sure to avoid straightening your back at this point, for if you do, you won't be able to roll.

When you feel comfortable with this, try starting in a standing position. Stand more or less at attention with your arms raised overhead. Then in one smooth motion bend your knees, elbows, and body into a squat position and go into your backward roll as before.

As long as you remember to finish each roll in the "ready" position, you'll have no problem doing three backward rolls in succession. As you arrive on your feet after the third roll, finish the stunt by pushing off and rising to a stand, arms once again straight overhead. Once you're stable, slowly lower your arms to your sides.

As you've probably noticed, a lot of tumbling tricks (and other gymnastics stunts) begin with arms raised overhead and end with the arms being lowered to your sides. There are a couple of reasons for this. Probably the most important is the fact that by raising your arms at first, you are signaling the judges and spectators that you are about to begin your performance. And by lowering them at the end, you are giving notice that you have finished. It's something like the final chord in a piece of music, and it shows everyone that you are in complete control of your body.

There's also the fact that you naturally end up in a raised arm position as you finish many stunts—the end position of a back handspring, for example, or a dismount from the high bar. And often this position provides a good lead-in for stunts that are to follow, making for a smooth transition from one trick to another. That's why it's a good idea to make these arm movements a habit by practicing them right from the start.

One of the biggest problems with this stunt is remaining in a tuck position from the time you begin your roll until you get your body over. If you allow yourself to unfold, you won't roll smoothly and will have trouble getting your legs to come over and down. Concentrate on using your stomach muscles to keep yourself tucked.

As you bring your body over your head, your elbows should stay in close to your body. Resist the urge to let them go out to the sides. Only by keeping them in close will you be in the strongest position to push from.

If you don't have enough speed to go over smoothly, you will probably need some help from your instructor.

Ask your instructor to stand near your feet at the beginning and walk forward as you rock up. He can then plant his feet on either side of you and, grabbing your hips, help lift you over. This will help you get the proper feel for the stunt. After a few assists, you'll probably be able to do it by yourself.

Begin by first doing the tucked head balance. Then slowly lift your knees one inch off your elbows. This will take a little weight shifting, so move very slowly until you have figured out what needs to be done. Your goal is to be able to balance in that position.

Once you can do that, reverse the order of your movements and come back down. Then lift your head off the mat, rock back into the standard squat, and take a rest. Then start again, running through the entire sequence until you are once more balanced with your knees an inch off your elbows. Now, very slowly, begin to push your feet up toward the ceiling. Push them until they are where you think is about halfway up. Then slowly lower them and return to the squat for a rest. Repeat this sequence two or three times until you can do it without shaking or wiggling.

You're almost there. But before moving on to a full headstand, it's important to learn how to do a forward roll from the tucked head balance. The reason for this is simple: If you go too high, too fast, in the next stage of the headstand, you'll lose your balance and come crashing down like a tree. Knowing how to go into a forward roll when you lose your balance will prevent that.

So, begin by going to the tucked head balance with knees an inch off the elbows, only while you're moving your legs, push the rest of your body up at the same time. The idea is to raise your body just enough to allow you to tuck your head under. Then simply go into a forward roll.

Headstand

As you bring your body over your head, your elbows should stay in close to your body. Resist the urge to let them go out to the sides. Only by keeping them in close will you be in the strongest position to push from.

Practice this several times. Try to make it something of a reflex action so that whenever you lose your balance in a headstand you do a forward roll almost without thinking.

Now you're ready to do a full headstand. Go to the tucked head balance with knees an inch off the elbows. Then slowly raise your legs all the way up until your toes are pointed at the ceiling. When you get to that position, slowly straighten out all the parts—knees, hips, and so on—until you are perfectly balanced.

This isn't easy, and it will take some practice. But doing a successful headstand is a major skill and well worth the effort.

The main problem people have when learning this stunt is that they try to move their bodies too fast. I can't emphasize it strongly enough: All motions must be slow so that you are on balance at all times. If you move too fast, you won't be able to shift your weight properly and you'll end up off balance. When this happens, don't panic. Simply go into a forward roll or return to the tucked head balance, whichever is easier. Don't try to shoot your feet up to the ceiling, hoping to regain your balance once you're upside down.

It may be a good idea to have someone stand next to you as you learn this trick. That way if you begin to fall over from the headstand position the spotter can grab your ankles, making sure you have enough time to get your head tucked for a forward roll.

THE HEADSTAND

a. From a tucked head balance, push your feet toward the ceiling until they are about halfway up.

b. Then slowly straighten out all the parts until you're on balance.

Backbridge

The backbridge is a very useful skill for several reasons. It's a basic tumbling position and it's a definite prerequisite for more advanced stunts like front and back handsprings. It's also a good warm-up exercise.

Begin by lying flat on your back. Bend your knees and bring your ankles up toward your seat. Put your hands behind your head, next to your ears, palms on the mat. Then push your stomach up toward the ceiling, straightening your arms and legs as you go. As you straighten your elbows, move your head back and down until you can see your hands on the floor.

When you first attempt this stunt, your feet should be about a shoulder's width apart. They should remain flat on the floor, pointed straight ahead. Later, after you feel comfortable forming the backbridge this way, try the more advanced version by doing it with your legs and ankles together.

If your shoulders and/or back are inflexible, you may not be able to do a backbridge right away. The solution is to do some stretching exercises before trying the stunt and to try doing a backbridge a few times each day until you gradually become more limber.

THE BACKBRIDGE

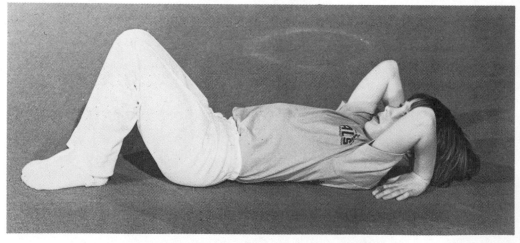

a. Begin in this position.

b. Push your stomach up toward
   the ceiling.

c. Straighten your elbows and
   move your head down until you
   can see your hands.

4
Floor Exercise

Most people don't know it, but the official worldwide name of the sport that's the subject of this book is "Artistic Gymnastics." If you think that implies creativity, imagination, and a little showmanship, you're absolutely right. These qualities are supposed to be a part of all gymnastic events, but nowhere are they more evident than in floor exercise.

Competitive floor exercise, or "floor-ex" or simply "floor," as it's often called, takes place on a mat in an area measuring twelve meters by twelve meters. The area is marked off with a white line, and the mat is usually large enough to allow about a one-foot margin all around. In international competition, you're allowed a maximum of seventy seconds in which to execute your routine, but you must perform for a minimum of fifty seconds.

A floor-ex routine itself consists predominately of tumbling skills linked together to form what the official rules call "a harmonious and rhythmical whole." Yet the objective of all floor-ex routines is to display a lot of other nontumbling skills as well. The general idea is to show all you can do with your body.

You can begin your routine anywhere within the area, but you are not allowed to step out of it until you are finished. You should use as much as possible of the approximately forty-foot by forty-foot floor area in all directions. And, as in all events except the long horse vault, you've got to fulfill an eleven-part requirement.

This means that somewhere in your routine you must do: one trick of superior difficulty, five intermediate tricks, and five tricks of lower difficulty. You've also got to alternate movements among those tricks involving things like balance, holding a position, strength, jumps, handsprings, and saltos (*salto* is the international word for somersault).

Gymnastics scoring is rather complex, but basically the maximum score you can earn is 10.0. As you perform your routine, fractions of a point are deducted from that total for one reason or another. These include things like imperfect execution of a stunt and faults like bad leg, foot, arm, head, or body position, and lack of balance.

Mistakes like these are usually pretty cut and dried, but there's also a subjective element in judging floor-ex. The thing to keep in mind is that floor exercise is first and foremost an artistic presentation and opinions vary on just what is artistic and what isn't. In general, though, you are supposed to make movements that are pleasing to the eye, and that usually means smooth motions, extended arms and legs, and making the difficult look easy. A gymnast should also appear to be light and as weightless as possible, and he should always move with a sureness that demonstrates complete mastery of his body.

A floor-ex routine should *flow,* with one stunt leading smoothly into another. And surprising as it may seem, it should have, as the rules put it, "a personal touch of expression and execution." That means you can add a jump here, a leap there, maybe a spin or two or anything else to express your personal flair.

Nor are you strictly limited in the stunts you are allowed to do. There may be compulsory routines at some meets, but they are almost always paired with an optional routine, meaning you perform twice. In optional routines, you're limited only by your own imagination. You can dream up any trick, and as long as you can do it smoothly and make it look interesting to the audience and judges, it has a valid place in floor exercise. In fact, coming up with a new trick is part of the challenge of being a top level gymnast.

So you steal a little bit from show business, a little from ballet, and even a little from the circus, and combine it with some good, solid tumbling skills, and you're all set. But don't let all the razzmatazz fool you. Floor exercise requires the most physical endurance of all the events. There you are on the mat, having to fill fifty to seventy seconds with some of the most difficult and demanding stunts you're capable of. You've got to demonstrate strength, flexibility, balance, and creativity and make it all look easy. Now that's a challenge you can really grab hold of.

So here we go. The stunts that follow are a little more difficult than those you've learned up until now. But if you've mastered the tricks in chapter 3, you shouldn't have any real problems. You can start linking stunts together to form miniroutines right from the start. I've provided a few suggestions, but feel free to use your imagination. At the end of the chapter you'll find a complete beginning floor-ex routine that uses many of the stunts in this and in the previous chapter.

Dive-Roll/Jump with Full Twist/Dive-Roll

Let's start with a sort of miniroutine. Here you'll learn to dive into a forward roll, come out of it rising to your feet, to a jump with a full twist, and dive into another forward roll. Be sure to use a four- to eight-inch-thick mat instead of a standard tumbling mat when learning this sequence.

Your first step should be to take a position similar to the one swimmers use just before the gun goes off at a swim meet. Stand with your legs slightly flexed and both arms out behind you. To start the action, swing your arms down and forward, keeping them parallel throughout, and place your hands on the mat about two feet in front of your own feet. Now straighten your knees and push off a little with your feet as you go into a forward roll.

Practice this basic move for a while and then gradually begin to swing your arms out farther so your hands land farther away from your feet. Work up to the point where you can give a little quicker push with your feet so that they leave the mat just as your hands make contact.

When this is working well for you, begin trying for more distance and more height. At this point, the push-off from your feet will become more like a jump, but remember to always catch your weight on your hands. Eventually you'll be completely in the air the moment before your hands touch down, and that's where the movement becomes a real dive-roll.

As you come out of the forward roll, you'll be on your feet in a squat. As you rise to a stand, raising your arms over your head, try to go a little faster than normal and do a jump and the half twist learned in chapter 3.

THE DIVE-ROLL

a. Begin from this position.

b. Swing your arms down and forward as you dive.

c. Straighten your knees and push off with your feet as you go into. . .

d. and through a forward roll.

When you can do that, make the half twist a full twist.

So much for the first part. Now we've got to add the second dive-roll. Assume that you've landed after doing your full twist. Your arms should stay up over your head, upper arms close to your ears. Now simply swing your arms rearward and down and then forward as you go into a half squat position. Then jump into another dive-roll. Work on this transition until you can do it smoothly, without stopping between the moment you land after the full twist and the time you begin moving into a half squat.

Be careful not to jump too high the first few times you do your full twist. If you do, you may land off balance and be unable to continue on into the lunge. Just start low and slow, adding speed and height after you've had some practice.

Handstands

Handstand Lead-Up

This is a stunt all by itself, but it's also a great way to prepare for stunts involving a full handstand. You begin by getting into the same position you'd use when beginning a push-up: palms on the mat, arms extended straight, legs straight, feet up on their toes. Bring one foot up closer to your hands, bending the knee. This will be your support leg.

HANDSTAND LEAD-UP (also called handstand stepdown)

a. You start in this position. . .

Now slowly lift your other leg—still keeping it straight with toes pointed—up off the mat.

To do this, you use the lunge position. Take your stand. Step forward into the lunge. Then slowly move down so that your hands are on the mat and you're in the beginning push-up position. Notice that the leg brought forward for the lunge will now be your support leg. Pause for a moment, and then bring your straight leg up and perform the stunt as before.

The pause is important at this stage because it counteracts the tendency to raise the straight leg too soon. Don't bring that leg up until your hands are properly placed on the mat. As you get better at the trick you can eliminate the pause and work toward a smoother execution. Just remember to take it slowly. Don't try to go too fast at first.

You may have to experiment a little until you learn how much strength is needed to keep your arms straight. By making sure that your arms are straight and that your shoulders are always directly over your hands, you'll not only have good form, you'll also make the trick easier. When your bones are lined up correctly, you can support yourself without much effort.

Keep your head in its original position at all times. Don't tuck it. You ought to be able to see your fingers and hands all during the stunt.

Finally, be sure not to go into a handstand. You want to come close to it but not completely into it.

b. and kick your straight leg up until you raise it to. . .

c. this angle, hold the position, and come back down.

Raise your straight leg a few inches at first, then return it to the floor. Repeat this leg lift with a bit more speed, trying to get it a little higher each time, until the momentum forces your support foot to lift off the mat slightly. When you've done that, try to hold your airborne position for a second before coming down. Then try to come down with your support foot in exactly the same spot.

The straight leg should be straight with toes pointed until it touches the mat. The idea is eventually to be able to get your straight leg up to the angle shown in the accompanying photograph, to hold the position very briefly, and then to come back down. However, you don't want to raise your leg so high that you pull yourself into a handstand.

Once you've mastered the trick with one leg, reverse positions and try it with the other leg as well. Then try getting into the stunt from a standing position.

Handstand

The stunt you've just learned is also called a "handstand stepdown," and that's how we'll refer to it from now on. Once you've mastered it, you'll be ready to move on to a complete handstand. To help you learn this stunt, it's a good idea to have a fellow student or your instructor standing by.

Begin by performing the handstand stepdown several times, trying to kick your straight leg higher each time. Then try to kick it high enough to pull the trunk of your body into a vertical position. The leg itself should stop somewhere past a vertical line drawn through your trunk, while your support leg rises to a spot about the same distance on the other side of that line. This is a split-leg position.

You should try to balance in the split-leg position for a moment. However, if you feel yourself falling back down, simply lower your rear leg and do a handstand stepdown. If you find that you've kicked your straight leg too far and are about to fall forward, your instructor or spotter will hold your legs to ease your landing.

Once you are able to balance in the split-leg position for about two seconds, try to join your legs together so that your whole body is vertical. By holding you in both this position and in the split-leg position, your instructor or spotter can help you get accustomed to the stunt and to what your muscles must do to perform it on their own.

When you've mastered the handstand and feel confident of your ability to perform it without assistance, practice beginning the stunt from a stand. From a stand, go into a lunge and lower yourself to the handstand stepdown position. Kick your straight leg up and follow with your support leg so that you're in the split-leg position. Then join your legs for a finished handstand. Complete the stunt by re-splitting your legs and performing a handstand stepdown.

Handstand–Forward Roll

It's also possible to get out of a handstand by going into a forward roll. In fact, linking these two stunts together can be very useful in a floor exercise routine, where it's important to keep moving in one direction or another as you cover the area.

With your instructor or a spotter standing by, do the handstand you just learned. Once you're balanced with your legs together overhead, the spotter will hold both your legs to help support some of your weight.

This will give you a chance to tuck your head, chin on chest, so that your shoulders are nearly touching the mat.

Now the spotter will lower you gently as you complete your tuck and go into a forward roll. You should come out of the roll as usual, arriving in a squat with hands up by your ears. Then you simply rise to a full stand.

The key to this stunt is to learn how and when to tuck your head before going into the roll. This will take some work, but as you get better at it, the instructor or spotter will gradually reduce his assistance until you can do it by yourself.

Once you can do a single handstand–forward roll, it's easy to do two

LEARNING THE HANDSTAND FORWARD ROLL

a. Once you're balanced in a handstand, someone can hold your legs and take some of the weight off your hands. . .

in a row. Begin the first handstand–forward roll by assuming the lunge position. Put your hands on the mat. Swing up to a handstand, joining the legs. Tuck your head and lower your shoulders. Do a forward roll up to your feet. Rise to a stand with arms overhead. Swing arms rearward, down and forward as you go into the lunge. Then repeat.

You'll probably have a tendency at first to try to do a forward roll before you've gotten yourself into a complete handstand. Do your best to resist it. If you try to do a forward roll before your legs are all the way up, you may literally fall flat on your face. So be mentally prepared to do the handstand stepdown if you try for a full handstand and don't make it. This will get you out of trouble safely.

b. giving you a chance to tuck your head and practice a forward roll.

Scale Balance or Front Scale

Balancing feats and tricks are a prime element of floor exercise competition. And while, by definition, they are all static positions, they are anything but easy to do. Most balanced positions or "scales" require a lot of strength and flexibility.

The front scale is a basic floor exercise stunt. You begin by standing with arms overhead and then step into the lunge position. At this point, a line drawn through your back leg, hips, shoulder, arm, and fingers should be absolutely straight. Now lift your rear leg off the floor, toes pointed, and try balancing on your bent leg.

When you can do that, try to straighten your bent leg as you tilt your body forward into a horizontal position. Your arms, of course, should also be horizontal, pointed out in front of you, and you should be looking straight ahead. With the exception of your support leg, your body will be in a sort of "Superman" flying position.

This isn't easy to do. But once you've become accustomed to the basic position, you should try to perfect it. Your goal should be to balance for several seconds with your rear leg, your hips, head, hands, and arms all in the same horizontal plane. As you practice, ask a friend

An acceptable front scale

to help you by standing back and telling you whether everything is lined up properly. Eventually you'll get so you will know whether or not you're on target just by the way it feels.

This is considered an acceptable front scale. However, there's a way to make it more difficult and possibly earn some bonus points in competition. (Judges usually subtract points for errors, but they are also permitted to add points for exceptional creativity or virtuosity.) Try the front scale as before, but this time hold the position with your rear leg, arms, and head raised *above* your hips and body. You'll have to bend your spine and your body will have to be very flexible to do this, so work up to it gradually.

You can come out of the front scale by lowering your rear leg and bringing yourself up to a stand. But you can also use it as a link to some other stunt. For example, you could bend your support leg slightly, put your hands on the mat, and go into a handstand–forward roll. Or, to make things even more elaborate, you could begin from a stand, lunge into a handstand–forward roll, come out of the roll rising to your feet and into a front scale, hold it for a few seconds, then go into another handstand–forward roll.

A front scale can be made more difficult by raising your rear leg, arms, and head even higher.

Forward Roll to a One-Legged Stand

Remember the part of the forward roll in which you're on your back, legs tucked, ready to come up to a squat? Well, instead of keeping both legs tucked, straighten one of them, pointing the toe, and try to arrive in a squat supported by the tucked leg. The straight leg will be out in front of you, and you'll look as though you're in the middle of a Russian dance.

Now for the really hard part. From this position try to straighten your support leg, rising to a stand, while keeping the straight leg out in front of you. This will demonstrate strength and flexibility and requires a lot of both.

Once you can do this, you can easily lean forward and touch down with your straight leg. By flexing the support leg at the same time, you'll find yourself in the lunge position, ready to go into some other stunt.

At first, getting up on one leg with the other held straight out in front will be hard enough. But you can make the stunt even more difficult by trying it with your arms held straight overhead and your front leg held even higher.

FORWARD ROLL TO A ONE-LEGGED STAND

a. Come out of a forward roll, arriving on one leg.

b. Then, holding the other leg out in front, rise to a stand.

THE BACKWARD EXTENSION ROLL

a. As you perform a backward roll, thrust your legs out and up until you can get your body straightened into a position near a handstand. Here as the gymnast comes out of a backward roll his legs are moving up and to the left as he pushes himself up with his hands to a near handstand.

Backward Extension Roll

The first step in learning this stunt is to do a backward roll but stop when you're exactly midway through it. You will be on your shoulders, legs and body tucked, hands on the mat by your ears. Now, instead of staying tucked, extend your legs so that they're pointing straight up toward the ceiling for a moment. Straighten your arms as much as possible and then land on your feet with your hands still on the floor.

Next, try the whole thing again, only this time thrust your legs out and up a little higher and harder and finish up as before. Practice this until you can get your body straightened up to a position *near* a handstand for a moment. Then bend at the waist and put your feet on the floor.

As a beginner, this is probably all you should do on this stunt at present. However, as you become more proficient, you'll want to be

b. After passing through
the handstand, bend at
the waist to put your feet
on the floor. Or do a
handstand stepdown.

able to execute a backward extension roll in its most desirable form. To
do this, you extend your legs and raise yourself to a full-fledged handstand, hold it for a moment, and then go into the handstand stepdown.

It's important to avoid going into a full handstand when you're
learning this trick. In fact, the first few times you extend your legs you
may not want to try for the halfway-between-ceiling-and-floor angle. In
the beginning, work on getting the feel of extending legs and
straightening elbows simultaneously so you can push your head off the
mat.

This trick will probably take a lot of strength at first. But as you
become more confident and add a little speed, the momentum of
extending your legs will help carry you up and the stunt will be more a
matter of coordination.

Cartwheels

Although considered a beginning stunt, a cartwheel is still a pretty impressive skill. It's a little difficult to do, so it's worth reemphasizing the importance of following the proper progression of steps as you learn it. Follow the steps just as they're presented here, and you'll be able to do the stunt safely without any problem.

We're going to learn two types of cartwheels and then see how to perform each type twice in a row. The first type begins with the lunge to a handstand stepdown you learned earlier. As you stand facing down the mat, try to picture yourself standing on a straight line running right out in front of you. Shift slightly to the right before starting, so that the line is next to your left foot. We'll assume you will be swinging your right leg up first, so as you go into a lunge, step forward with your left leg.

Lunge down as though you were going to do a handstand, but plant your left hand on that imaginary line. Your right hand should be planted about a shoulder's width from your left. This means you'll shift slightly to the right as you lunge. Swing your right leg up and then bring up your left leg. You'll be in a handstand, but your legs should be split, right leg leaning forward, left leg leaning back. If you find you can't make the split-leg handstand at first, then just ease back down onto your left leg and try again.

When you arrive at the handstand, begin to lean forward a bit. Quickly pick up your right hand and plant it on the line about a shoulder's width in front of your left hand. You'll pivot slightly on your left hand as your body twists around.

Next, put your right leg on the line even farther out than your right hand. You'll be moving it down and sideways and the action will tend to pull your body upright. You can help things along by pushing off a little with your left hand. The left leg, of course, follows naturally and should also be placed on the line.

The explanation takes a lot longer than the stunt itself. And while the trick doesn't look like a cartwheel yet, mastering it is an important preliminary step.

The next step is to stand with your left foot on the imaginary line. Lunge forward and plant your left hand on the line in front of your left foot. Be sure to keep your right arm stretched out above your left arm. Now swing your right leg up and *at the same time* place your right hand on the line. You'll pivot slightly on your left hand as before.

A CARTWHEEL DONE FROM A LUNGE

a. Lunge forward on your left leg.

b. Plant your left hand on the imaginary line (a piece of tape in this picture) and your right hand about a shoulder's width away.

d. Plant your right hand on the
   line, pivoting on the left hand.

c. You'll be in a handstand with
   legs split.

e. Move your right leg down and sideways as you push off with your left hand. You'll land in a lunge, facing back the way you came. Your right leg will now be the forward leg, making it easy to do a cartwheel back to your original position.

See if you can swing your right leg all the way through—past the vertical position so that it's in front of you—and place it on the line. This will look more like a real cartwheel.

Now push off with your left hand and then with the right. Bring your left leg down and onto the line and pivot so that you are facing back the way you came. Notice that your right leg will now be the forward leg. This makes it easy to again go into a lunge and do another cartwheel. Only this time, you'll start by planting your right hand on the line and swinging your left leg up first.

When you've done this sequence a number of times, you'll be ready for the complete trick. Begin with arms overhead, step forward into a lunge with your *left* leg, pass smoothly through the lunge and into a cartwheel. You will end up in a lunge position facing back the way you came. Instead of holding that pose, straighten up and step back onto your rear (left) foot and join your legs. Your hands will still be over your head. From here go right into a lunge, stepping forward with your *right* leg and do another cartwheel.

This is a perfectly acceptable miniroutine often used in floor-ex competition. Usually it doesn't matter which cartwheel (right leg or left leg) you execute first, so long as you demonstrate both of them.

The second type of cartwheel is the one most people think of when they hear the word. It's easy to learn once you've mastered the handstand type. Begin by standing, arms overhead, with your left side to the imaginary line. Swing your left leg straight out to the left and plant it on the line. Then quickly bring your left arm and shoulder down so you can plant your left hand about eighteen inches farther along the line than your foot. You'll have to flex at the waist, and the movement will bring your right leg up off the mat. Try to keep your arms and legs rather stiff.

Next place your right hand on the line about a shoulder's width from your left hand. While you're doing this, keep your eyes focused on the mat on a spot between your hands. Moving your right arm into position

A SECOND KIND OF CARTWHEEL

a. Swing your left leg out and place
   it on the line.

b. Bend at the waist as you plant
   your left hand on the line.

c. Keep your eyes focused on a spot between your hands as you bring your right leg up. . .

d. and through. Bring your right leg down onto the mat and arrive in a stand with your arms overhead.

will help you bring your right leg up and through. And that will help you bring up your left leg.

Finish up by pushing off a little with your left hand and bringing your right leg down and onto the line. Again, keep your arms and legs stiff so you can use them like the spokes of a wheel. You should arrive in a stand with your arms over your head, which makes it very easy to continue with another cartwheel in the same direction or do one that will carry you back the way you came.

Either type of cartwheel is acceptable for competition, unless you must do a compulsory routine that specifies a certain type. The second type, though, is better suited for continuing on in the same direction— as when you're doing a series of stunts that carry you across the mat.

Speed and momentum can be a big help in getting your body up, over the top, and down on the other side. But try to go slowly at first. You don't, for instance, have to hurry through the lunge position when doing the first type of cartwheel. Just try to make it a smooth motion at first. You can add some speed later. And remember, you want to eventually be able to execute both types of cartwheels in both directions equally well.

The Roundoff

The roundoff is a key stunt in floor-ex because it can be used to convert a forward run into a backward movement. It begins like the cartwheel and can be done to either side. Here we'll learn it from a standing position and going to the right.

Begin as in a cartwheel, by imagining yourself straddling an invisible line running down the mat. Step into a lunge with your left foot and, bending at the waist, plant your left hand on the line. Follow with your right hand as you swing your right leg up into the air. The fingers of your left hand should cross the line at a right angle, but your right hand should point more or less back toward the direction you were lunging from.

This will cause your body to twist as in a cartwheel, and as this happens bring your left leg up to join your right. You'll now be in a handstand, legs together, directly above the line.

To complete the stunt, bring your legs down so that they land on the line with toes pointing back toward the place you began. Your body will thus twist some more as you come down to stand facing the opposite direction from which you started.

In its final form, the stunt should be done smoothly from beginning to end. That is, you should pass through the handstand without holding the position. Once you can do a roundoff in one direction, go on and perfect it in the other direction. You may also want to work on connecting the roundoff to another stunt by immediately going into a backward roll at the finish.

THE ROUNDOFF
a. Bend forward to plant your left hand on the line.
b. Your left hand should cross the line at a right angle, while right hand points back the way you came. This causes your body to twist. (In a simple handstand, of course, both hands point as the left hand does here.)
c. Complete the stunt by bringing your legs down with toes pointing back toward your starting position.

a.

b.

c.

The Hurdle

The hurdle is simply a little skip step taken at the beginning of a stunt to give yourself a little speed. Begin by standing with your arms at your sides. Then raise your arms straight forward and up until they're overhead. At the same time, raise your left leg, knee straight and toes pointed. Done with enough speed, the momentum of these two actions will help pull you into a forward skip on your right foot.

As your right foot hits the mat after the skip, step down with your left foot and go into a cartwheel or a roundoff. You'll probably find that the little extra forward motion provided by the hurdle makes these stunts a bit easier.

When you're comfortable doing the hurdle, try adding a little step. Step forward with your right foot and as you bring your left leg forward, raise your arms and do a hurdle. Then go into a cartwheel or a roundoff. This will further increase your speed.

The hurdle

If you like, you can add two more steps as well. But you'll have to stop there since in gymnastics even the most difficult tumbling stunts are never preceded by more than three steps and a hurdle. Be sure to learn the hurdle and steps on both legs.

Two One-Handed Cartwheels

It seems that a stunt is no sooner invented than someone comes up with a way to make it more challenging. But then that's the fun of gymnastics. The one-handed cartwheel is a case in point.

Here we'll use the type of cartwheel done from a lunge. Stand next to the imaginary line. Lunge onto your left leg and place your left hand on the line. Then kick over so quickly that you don't have to put your right hand on the mat and, pushing off with your left hand, land in a lunge (right leg forward) facing the opposite direction. Repeat the trick by going back that way and using your right hand instead of your left. This is called a near arm cartwheel.

The secret is to swing your first leg (the right one when doing it to the left) up and over much faster than in a two-handed cartwheel. You need the momentum to carry you over. It's also important to swing that leg straight up and over the top so that you land straight on the line. If you swing crooked, you'll land off balance.

At first, keep your right hand near the floor. That way you can use it if you have to. But later, if you really want to fancy up the stunt, try to keep your right arm stretched out to the side.

This is a difficult trick for most people. But once you can perform it, you might want to make it more difficult still. Begin the trick by placing both hands *near* the line at the same time. Then, when the left hand is only an inch from the mat, take it away and use your right hand instead. You should place your right hand on the spot that would otherwise be occupied by your left hand as you swing your left arm away to the side. You'll then be doing a cartwheel on your far arm, and you'll have to move even more quickly than before to get your body over.

When doing a far arm cartwheel, you'll probably want to take your left arm away too soon. Counteract this tendency by concentrating on putting both hands near the line at the same time. This is also a good safety measure since your left hand will be there to help if you don't have enough speed to complete the trick on one hand.

Be sure to practice the one-handed cartwheel in either direction, and work on a smooth transition between the first and second cartwheels in the sequence.

Headspring

The last trick we'll learn for now requires a lot of flexibility, and you shouldn't attempt it until you have enough to do a good backbridge. Also, the stunt should be learned on a soft mat instead of the competition tumbling mat.

Start in a squat and put your hands on the mat in front of you. Then place your head on the mat just as if you were going to do the tucked head balance learned in chapter 3. Only this time, don't put your knees on your elbows. Instead, keeping your toes on the mat, straighten your knees.

Slowly move your hips over your head so that your toes come four to six inches off the mat. Gradually try to raise your legs farther. Practice this move until you can balance on your head and hands with your legs perfectly straight and nearly horizontal.

Next, get into this balance position, hold it for a moment, and then move your hips forward so that you just begin to fall over onto your back. At that point, swing your legs over your body and put your feet on the floor. Straighten your elbows and put yourself into the backbridge position.

Once you can do this, try to move a little faster as you bring your legs over from the balance position. Try pushing up with your arms as your legs come over. It will take some work, but eventually you'll find yourself pushing hard enough to shift your weight onto your feet. Your momentum will then help raise your body to a standing position.

Good speed and a strong push with your hands and arms are the secrets to this stunt. It's also important to keep your head bent back so that your eyes will be looking at your hands (as in a regular backbridge) all the time. The body is arched and you lead with your stomach and hips as you come up onto your feet. You'll come out of the stunt standing on your feet, stomach out and back arched, arms and head bent back. Then you simply straighten up into a regular stand.

a. Practice until you can balance in this position.

b. Then move your hips forward until you just begin to fall over onto your back.

c. Swing your legs over your body. . .

d. and put your feet on the floor, pushing up with your arms as your legs come over.

e. With enough speed, you'll be able to raise your body. . .

f. to a stand. Note: This stunt has been photographed on a padded floor exercise area. But when learning how to do it, you should use a mat softer than the competition tumbling mat.

A Complete Floor Exercise Routine

This routine is made up of the stunts you've already learned. It's designed to cover all parts of the floor, to be what is considered "harmonious," and to include alternating elements of balance, hold, strength, and flexibility. Depending upon how proficient you are, it should even fit within the fifty- to seventy-second time limit.

You could take this routine into competition if you wanted to. But you should probably use it as a starting point, something to be customized to your own specifications. You can get a lot of good ideas for additional stunts and little touches by asking your instructor and by watching others compete at gymnastics meets.

1. Stand in one corner so that the border of the area is immediately to your left. (We'll call that border side 1—see diagram.)

2. Raise your arms overhead to signal you're ready to begin.

3. Step into a cartwheel. (Perform whichever kind of cartwheel you you can do best.)

4. Do a second cartwheel, either of the same type used·in step 3 or one of a different type, if you can do it well.

5. As you come out of this cartwheel, do a quarter twist so that you finish facing back at your starting position. Side 1 will now be on your right.

6. Place both hands on the floor in front of you and swing one leg up to a near handstand.

7. As you approach a handstand, bring up your other leg and join it to the first leg. At the same time, do a quarter twist to the right by moving your left hand and pivoting on your right.

8. Step down from the near handstand onto one foot and do a half twist in place. (You will now be facing down side 2.)

9. Step into a handstand–forward roll.

10. Do a second handstand–forward roll, ending in a squat.

11. Place hands on mat and do a tuck head balance.

12. Hold that position for two seconds, the official requirement for balance parts.

13. Then roll forward (*slowly*) to a seated position with your legs straight. (Note: If you are rolling out of a headstand balance, be sure to lift your body and tuck your head as you start the roll.)

14. Demonstrate your flexibility by either touching your toes with your fingers or by grasping your ankles and lowering your chest to touch your legs. Knees straight, of course.

15. Swing arms up overhead and execute a backward extension roll. Come down from the momentary handstand by landing on your right foot.

16. Push off with your hands and, balancing on that foot, do a front scale. Hold for two seconds.

17. As you lower your left leg, do a five-eighths twist to the left. (Don't worry about the fraction. The idea is to twist around so you're facing down the area's diagonal, leading back to your starting position.)

18. Take a single step forward and a hurdle as you go into a dive-roll.

19. Come out of the dive-roll and into a jump in place with a full twist.

20. Do a second dive-roll.

21. As you come out of it, do a jump in place with a three-eighths twist to the left. You'll now be facing down side 4.

22. Step into a roundoff.

23. As you come out of it, go into a tucked backward roll.

24. Follow this with a back extension roll.

25. Stepdown and drop to a squat.

26. Then immediately leap up, arms raised, and do a jump with a half or full twist.

27. You'll arrive at a stand with arms overhead. Hold the position for just a second; then lower your arms, signalling the end of the routine.

Diagram of Floor Exercise Routine

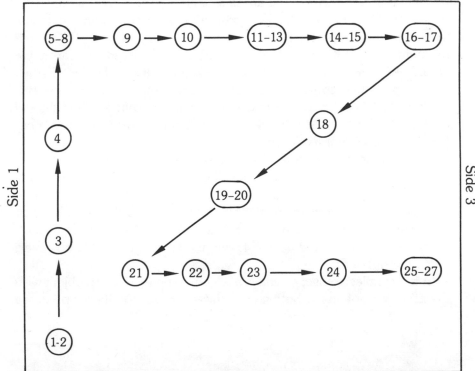

5
The Long Horse Vault

If you've ever vaulted over a fence or a fallen log or played leapfrog when you were younger, you know how much fun it can be. In fact, vaulting is probably the one event with which you've had the most experience outside the gym, possibly even more than with tumbling.

That's not surprising, for vaulting is a pretty natural human movement, one that people have been executing and enjoying for literally thousands of years. In the ancient Mediterranean kingdom of Crete, for instance, there was a very popular exhibition sport called bull leaping. As the crowds in the arena looked on, the athlete would walk up to the bull and place his hands on its head just behind the horns. Timing his moves precisely, the athlete would kick his feet at the same moment the bull began to toss its head as it prepared to charge. He would then somersault onto the bull's back and leap off behind its tail.

That particular sport died out over three thousand years ago. But vaulting itself lives on today, only now we use an artificial horse instead of a live bull. Officially the event is the "long horse vault," but most gymnasts refer to it as "vaulting."

The long horse is exactly the same piece of equipment as the side horse, except that the pommels have been removed. But not everyone vaults over it lengthwise. Gymnasts who are twelve years old and younger vault over from one side to another. Older people vault lengthwise, but not always with the horse at the same height. Generally, the older the gymnast, the higher the horse. All, however, use a springboard.

In the simplest sense, a vault is a way of jumping over an object with the assistance of one or both hands. Indeed, in competition, points are deducted for touching the horse with your foot or any other part of your body.

Yet the vault itself isn't the main point of the event. The essence of the long horse vault is flight—from the springboard to the horse (preflight) and from the horse to the landing (postflight). Between them the gymnast does what is basically a handspring or a cartwheel.

Flight requires height, and height requires speed. So the rules allow you to start your approach anywhere within twenty meters of the end of the horse. The rules also require you to land in perfect control of your body. Naturally, you are expected to flex your knees to absorb the shock of landing. But you're not supposed to squat too far, take a step or do anything else demonstrating lack of balance.

Within this overall framework, a gymnast can do a lot of different things to make his vault more difficult and impressive. During the preflight, for instance, it's possible to do a half or full twist. On the way down, during the postflight, twists, saltos (of many varieties), and other maneuvers are possible.

A gymnast is scored on the basis of his performance in each of the two flight components. The rules assign each vault a particular level of difficulty for each age group and stipulate the maximum number of points it's possible to earn for each one. The higher the difficulty level, the higher the points, up to a maximum of 10.0.

The long horse vault is the only event that does not have an eleven-part requirement regarding the number and difficulty of the stunts a competitor must perform. This is because the vault is really just one stunt. That makes the long horse vault the dragstrip of gymnastics! It calls for a single burst of lightning-fast reflexes and then it's over.

You get one shot and that's it. If you make a mistake in the other events, you usually have time to recover and continue with your routine. Sure, you'll lose some points, but you won't wipe out your score. In the long horse, the whole thing is over before you have a chance to recover.

The rules differ from one organization to another, but usually gymnasts are given only one vault. In large, high-level contests, such as the National Collegiate Athletic Association (N.C.A.A.) Championships or the Olympics, finalists may be required to do two different vaults and have the results averaged for their final scores. Rules also differ on whether a gymnast may specialize in vaulting, performing in only this and possibly one other event. This may be permitted if an organization wants to encourage as many people to participate as possible. But the overall trend is toward requiring gymnasts to compete in all six Olympic events.

In the Beginning

There are two important things to remember if you are just now learning to vault. First, safety mats, and second, beginning with side horse vaults instead of long horse vaults.

In the landing area, you should have at the very least a four-inch mat. However, *two* four-inch mats is a more acceptable minimum.

Even if your age requires you to compete on the long horse, it's important to start out vaulting over the side of the horse. This will help you get a feel for the apparatus, and it will allow you to concentrate on developing the skills you'll need when you move to the long horse. The side horse should be set at about waist level at first. As you become more proficient at the following vaults, gradually raise the horse to stomach and then to chest level. Heights used in competition, as mentioned earlier, vary with the age group. But at the highest level, the horse will be set at fifty-three inches. Be sure to master each vault going to the left and to the right when possible.

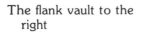

The flank vault to the right

Flank Vault

Stand facing the side of the horse and place both hands on it as you jump up with both feet. Swing your legs over the horse to the right side and land facing your original direction. To allow your body to pass over the horse, you'll have to release your right hand before your left.

Like many stunts, this vault is named for the part of your body that comes closest to the horse as you pass over it. In this case it was your side or flank.

Be sure to do the trick going to your left as well. If you like, you can also add a little two- or three-step approach.

Front Vault

Now try the same vault, only this time add a little twist so that your front passes over the horse, instead of your flank. Do the twist just as you are releasing the first hand. Leave the second hand on the horse and land with either your left or right side to the horse.

Next, do the same stunt but try to land so that you're facing the horse when you land. Your hands will have to exchange places, but they should both be on the horse as you land. Practice the stunt going to both sides.

Finally, do the same stunt you just learned, but try to continue twisting so that you land with your left side to the horse (assuming you're going over on the left) instead of your front. You'll have added an extra quarter twist and will have to release your right hand and hold it out to the side while you do it. Land with your left hand on the horse and your right arm held straight out to the right side.

The front vault to the right. The gymnast
is moving toward the camera.

Variation of the Flank Vault

This stunt will prepare you for doing the rear vault which follows. We'll assume you're going over the horse to the left.

Perform the flank vault learned earlier, but as you release your right hand (the first to be released) twist to the right so that you land with your right side to the horse. Your right hand should be on the horse.

Rear Vault

Do this one the easy way first. Stand with both hands on the horse and swing your legs up and over on the right as you would for a flank vault. However, while you're in the air over the horse, twist to your

THE REAR VAULT

a. Just after the twist to the right and. . .

right, releasing first your right and then your left hand. Land in a sitting position on the horse. Then simply slide off.

Now try it with a little more speed. Do the same twist to right as above, but don't sit on the horse. You'll release your right hand first and start it swinging back and to the right. Then you'll release your left hand and put your left arm straight out to your side. You'll twist as your bottom crosses the horse and regrasp with your right hand, landing with your right side to the horse.

This is a basic rear vault. Once you've got it down, you can make it more difficult by continuing your twist so that you land facing the horse. Or you can make it even more difficult by adding yet another quarter twist so that you finish with your left side to the horse.

b. the landing.

Squat on/Jump off

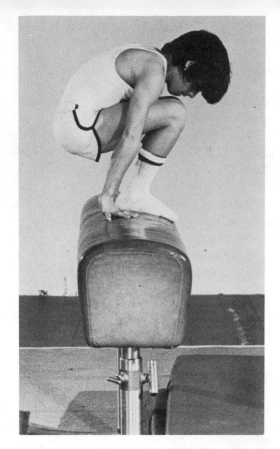

Squat On/Jump Off

This isn't a real vault, but it is a vaulable skill to learn as preparation for the stoop vault. Before you begin, get into a pushup position on the floor and practice snapping your legs up into a squat with your hands still on the mat. This is basically the same movement you'll be doing on the horse.

Next, make sure the horse is still at waist level and place your hands in the center of the apparatus a little more than a shoulder's width apart. Then jump up with both feet and land on the horse in a squat, feet between your arms. From this position, pick up your hands and push off with your feet as you jump down on the other side.
on the other side.

You should have an instructor or spotter helping you with this stunt in case you don't get your feet on the horse or in case they slip off. Also, be careful not to bring your feet through without touching the horse, since you would land with both arms still on the horse and stretched out behind at a painful angle.

As you become more confident, try adding more stretch to your jump off the horse. Jump up as straight as you can, thrusting your arms overhead and keeping them there as you land on both feet. You should bend at the knees to cushion the shock of landing, but right from the start you should work on control. Try to land without having to take an extra step or being off balance, pause for a moment, then lower your arms to your sides.

As you get better and better, add a variation or two. Try doing a half twist in the air before landing. And then try for a full twist. Later you can add a short run and try to bring your legs through without touching the horse. This means you'll be going over the horse in a squat vault, and the caution about allowing your arms to remain back on the horse is the same as before. Be sure to push off with your hands as you leave the horse, stretch your body to its full length, and raise your arms overhead.

Straddle Vault

With the horse set at waist level, jump up to a "straddle stand." In this position, your hands will be on the center of the horse and you'll have

The straddle vault

one leg on either side of them. Hold that position, then push up with your arms and gently jump off the horse, bringing your legs together as you land.

As you learn this skill, you should have an instructor or spotter stand on the far side of the horse. There the spotter can grab your upper arm to help lift you off the horse if necessary. This is in case your feet get stuck up on the horse and you begin to fall forward toward a landing on your head.

When you can execute both the straddle stand and jump off, put the two movements together into a smooth motion without a pause in the middle.

Using the Springboard

Up to now, you've been doing everything either from a stand or from a short run. You may or may not have been using a springboard. At this point, however, it's important to learn how to use one properly. As you may have already discovered, a springboard is unlike any other device you've ever jumped from. Nowhere near as bouncy as even the stiffest diving boards, a springboard is designed to provide a short, quick, concentrated lift, and there's a special technique for using one.

You run to the board and jump onto it with both feet. The jump must be as low and quick as you can make it, and your knees and ankles should be only *slightly* bent. Because of the way the spring is conveyed to your body, your legs must be very tense. If they're too flexible, the spring won't be able to travel up and into your body. You should hit the board on the toes and balls of your feet.

To get used to the board, place it so that you can stand up on it and reach out to touch the horse without bending at the waist. Approach the board with a gentle three- to five-step run and try the vaults learned earlier. As you become more confident, you can circle your arms up to get a little extra height, and you can raise the horse to a higher setting.

Stoop Vault

The stoop is a lot like the squat vault except that you raise your hips higher and keep your legs straight. Move the springboard back a little before beginning. Do your take-off and as you reach for the horse with your hands, begin to raise your hips so that they will be above your head by the time your hands make contact. You'll be at the beginning of a pike position.

Next, push up and off the horse with your arms and bring your legs through as you continue forward over the horse. You might think of it as doing a jackknife over the horse. Be sure to start with the apparatus at a relatively low setting.

At first, try to land as best you can. But later you should try to extend your body completely as you come out of the pike and raise your arms overhead. You'll then land in a standing position.

The stoop vault: Raise your hips over your head as you reach for the horse.

Learning the Handspring Vault

Now let's put the horse aside for a while and learn how to go over upside down, that is, in a handspring. As I mentioned earlier, the handspring is the basic skill of the long horse vault. Nearly everything else is a variation of it created by adding twists during the preflight and assorted saltos and twists during the postflight.

We'll learn the handspring on mats first, and we'll follow a gradual progression designed to make it as easy and safe as possible. Please be sure to follow this progression carefully. Don't jump ahead. If you master each phase along the way, you'll finish up with a skill you can be proud of and a confidence in your ability to perform it.

The first thing you should do is build a vaulting object out of folded tumbling mats. When folded, each mat will be about a foot thick. Stack

a. If you don't have enough thick mats, you can arrange tumbling mats like this. . .

the folded mats one on top of the other to form an object two or three feet high, two feet wide, and six feet long. The height of the object can be modified to suit your own height. We'll use this like a horse and refer to it as the "v.o." (vaulting object).

Next, build up your landing area on the far side of the v.o. Use at least a twelve-inch mat on top of an eight-inch mat. Two or three twelve-inch mats stacked together would be better still. The idea is to raise the landing area to almost the same height as the v.o.

If all of these mats aren't available, there are some easy ways to accomplish the same thing. You could place two additional folded tumbling mats about two feet apart so that they form a U with the v.o. at its base, and cover these with both a four-incher and an eight-incher. Or you could use a good strong table or stage risers covered with the same combination of mats or with a twelve-inch mat.

b. and cover them with a four-incher and an eight-incher.

Doing It by the Numbers

With your vaulting object and landing area all in place, put the springboard a comfortable distance in front. Now you can begin.

1. With hands on the v.o. and feet on the board, step into a single leg swing up to a near handstand. Do the stepdown as you did in tumbling.

2. Try the same stunt with two legs, bringing them both up together. You won't be able to go as high as in step 1, and you may want to try it with the v.o. at two feet (just remove the top mat) at first. Bring your legs back down to a stand.

These two steps teach you how to come back down safely. It's a skill worth working on, for you will use it even at the most advanced levels.

3. With the v.o. at two feet, swing one leg up to a near handstand. Join the second leg to it and do a quarter twist to the left. This is just like learning how to do a cartwheel. You twist by moving the left hand over and placing it in front of the right. Land on the other side of the v.o. on one foot or one knee. Practice until you can do the handstand, go through the twist, and do a controlled landing on both feet.

4. Execute step 3 as before, only do it from a jump off of both feet. Jump up and land with your hands on the v.o. and your legs in a squat above you. Straighten your legs to a full handstand. Twist and land as before.

Don't even think about continuing with the twist and landing until you are sure you're balanced in a handstand or already past the vertical on your way down to a landing. (In the latter case, you'd want to twist to keep from flopping flat on your back.) In other words, don't try to twist too soon. If you attempt a handstand and see that you aren't going to make it, come back to the board. Then try again.

5. With the v.o. at two feet, the landing mats should be higher than the v.o. And that's an ideal setup for learning how to land on your back from a handstand. Perform the full handstand as before, but instead of twisting, allow yourself to fall over onto your back. You

should land with straight legs, arms overhead, and head looking back at the v.o. Concentrate on looking at your hands the entire time.

6. Now add a folded mat to make the v.o. three feet high and move the springboard back a little. Take a short run and jump into a handstand on the v.o. You may want to work up to this gradually by repeating the previous steps with the board in its new position. At this point, always step down out of the handstand without going all the way over. Eventually you'll get to where you're doing a little flying from board to v.o.

7. Do a handstand as in step 6, but finish it by pushing off with your arms as your body crosses the vertical position. The combination of this push and your forward momentum should carry you to a landing one to two feet from the v.o. Your body should land as in step 5: legs straight, arms overhead, eyes looking back at the v.o.

8. Execute step 7, but instead of landing on your back, use your tumbling log roll to twist over onto your stomach before you hit the mat. Here's a word of caution, though: Don't twist unless you are quite certain you can land perfectly flat. If you land on your stomach with one end of your body higher than the other, your back will bend, and that can be painful.

9. Do step 8, but try for a full twist so that you land on your back.

10. With the board a little closer and the v.o. at three feet, do a gentle jump to a handstand. However, land in the backbridge you learned in tumbling. Practice thoroughly.

11. Remove one twelve-inch landing mat (or its equivalent) and execute step 10. Then remove a second twelve-inch mat and repeat. The landing area will now be two feet lower, and you may find that your hands will automatically come off the v.o. as your feet touch down. If they don't, push off a little until they do.

12. Now you're ready to move the board back a bit. Take a few steps, hit the board, and fly toward the v.o. and into a handstand. Then push off as in step 11 so that you also fly out of this position and up onto your feet.

You've just done the basic handspring used in vaulting.

DOING IT BY THE NUMBERS

a. Step 1. Swing up to a
near handstand and
step down.

b. Step 3. From a near
handstand. . .

c. do a quarter twist to the left. . .

d. and land on both feet.

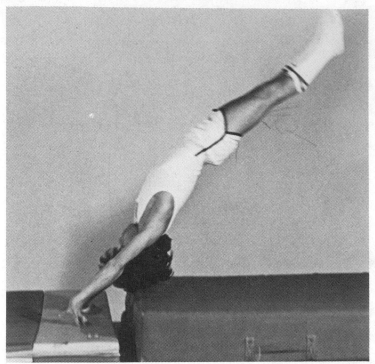

e. Let yourself fall onto your back from a handstand.

f. Step 6. Flying toward the v.o.

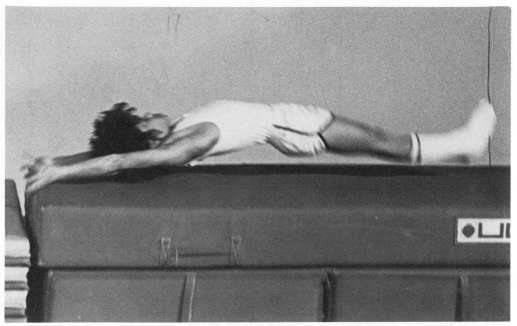

g. Step 7. Push off from a handstand so that you land on your back, farther from the v.o. than in Step 5.

h. Step 10. With the landing area and the v.o. at the same height, go into a backbridge from your handstand.

i. Step 11. Then do a backbridge with the landing area 12 inches lower.

j. Step 12. Leaving the v.o. and flying to a. . .

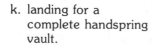

k. landing for a complete handspring vault.

Where Do We Go from Here?

You should use just the twelve-inch landing mat from now on, but add a fourth folded tumbling mat to the vaulting object. This will bring the v.o. nearer to the height of the horse used for beginning competition. Practice your handspring at this new height by first moving the board in close. As you get better at it, gradually move the board farther away so you can do more flying.

The next step is obviously to bring back the horse and to try to apply your new skill to that apparatus. Start low, with the springboard in close. The surface of the horse won't give as much as the softer v.o., so you'll have to adjust. You may also want to build up the landing area with more mats. But normally it doesn't take too long to transfer the skill from v.o. to horse.

You can learn the handspring on the v.o. pretty much by yourself. But when you move to the horse, you should have an instructor's help. The instructor probably will have you follow the same pattern used to learn the skill on the mats, with horse low and board in close at first, then a gradual increase of board distance and horse height.

The Long Horse

It's easy to learn a handspring on the long horse once you've mastered it on the side horse. You might want to begin as before by creating a vaulting object out of folded tumbling mats. This time, however, make it into a long object. Start with three stacked folded mats next to three twelve-inch landing mats. Pull the top landing mat back and rotate the top folded mat forty-five degrees so that you look at it lengthwise as you stand in front of the v.o. This will give you a six-foot-long, three-foot-high "horse" to practice on, with plenty of padding in the landing area.

Because it's longer, you'll need more speed in the approach than before. So take from seven to ten steps. Place your hands on the v.o. wherever comfortable at first, but work toward eventually being able to place them at the far end. Finally, use this setup to practice all of the exercises and handsprings learned while mastering the side horse handspring (steps 1 through 12).

PRACTICING THE LONG
HORSE VAULT

a. Flight

b. Contact

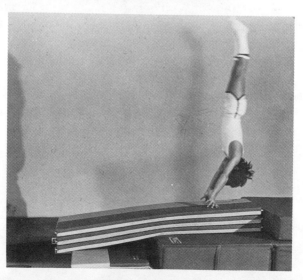

c. Handspring

A Word about Competition

As mentioned earlier, younger gymnasts compete by vaulting over the side horse. But at beginning levels, older people may do stoop, squat, straddle, and other basic vaults over the long horse.

I think that's fine, but if you're a beginner and are eligible for the long horse, I think there's a good chance you could learn a long horse handspring relatively quickly. Of course, you'll probably have to work on it a season or so before you're ready to take it into competition. But if you follow the steps I've given you and master each one before moving on to the next, you may well be perfecting your handspring while your competitors are just learning theirs.

With a good handspring to your credit, you'll be in a good position to move on (with the help of an instructor) to saltos and twists and other advanced skills.

6
The Horizontal Bar

In the early nineteenth century a young German named Frederick Ludwig Jahn (1778–1852) conceived an idea that was to have a tremendous impact upon his life and upon the sport of gymnastics. Struck by the tremendous potential gymnastics held for developing the human body, Jahn could see no reason why gymnastics shouldn't be available to everybody. Jahn envisioned an entire nation of physically fit citizens and toward that end he developed a system of *turnen* (gymnastics) that later became the basis of the *Turnverein* or turner societies that are still active today.

A firm believer in fresh air and outdoor activity, Jahn also opened a specially constructed *turnplatz* (athletic field) in Berlin in 1811. The idea quickly spread, and soon there were many such fields throughout the country.

These exercise fields boasted all of the latest gymnastics apparatus of the day. But Jahn was always thinking of ways to improve his system, and he would frequently come up with exercises for which there was no standard piece of apparatus.

That never stopped him, though. Whenever there was a need, he simply invented the required piece of equipment. Over the course of his career, Jahn introduced the parallel bars, the horizontal bar, and the balance beam (now used in women's gymnastics), as well as a substantially improved pommel horse.

These inventions, plus his system of exercises and his lifelong dedication to the sport, made Frederick Ludwig Jahn a major figure in the history of physical fitness. They are also the reasons he is widely considered the "Father of Gymnastics."

Jahn is said to have gotten the idea for the horizontal bar from watching children swing on tree limbs. That's not surprising since, as I've said before, many gymnastics events have their roots in nawtural physical activities. In fact, even newborn babies instinctively grasp at objects, and pulling themselves up with their arms is one of the first skills they learn.

The modern high bar, however, is a far cry from tree limbs and crib toys. A precision piece of equipment, the horizontal bar is a solid spring steel bar measuring 94 1/2 inches long and 1 1/10 inches in diameter. The bar is held 102 inches above the floor by two steel uprights that are inserted in floor plates and secured with cables and turnbuckles or steel support rods.

It may be hard to believe until you try it, but the bar is meant to bend about four inches when in use and spring back when no one's touching it. The bar makes a great amount of spring and lift possible, and this flexibility can be an important factor in many advanced stunts.

Most high bars are adjustable and can be lowered to chest or shoulder height. This is essential when learning many new stunts, and if the bar at the gym you're considering *isn't* adjustable you should probably look someplace else. You should also pay particular attention to the mats on the floor beneath, behind, and in front of the bar. Hopefully there will seem to be mats everywhere. This is a key point because you've got to face the fact that as you practice you may sometimes lose your grip on the bar.

At the minimum, you should have three twelve-foot long, eight-foot wide tumbling mats laid end to end. That will give you a strip thirty-six feet long, and it should be centered under the bar. Four mats (for a total of forty-eight feet) would be even better. On top of this strip should be two four-inch thick mats (or one eight-incher) on the front side and two on the back.

This arrangement is fine for learning, but it won't be adequate once you really begin to swing on the bar. At that level of skill, and preferably at the beginning as well, you should have the protection of two thirty-six-foot strips of four-inch mats laid on top of each other. That will require six twelve by eight mats four inches thick in all and give you eight inches of padding.

Chalking up and Preparing the Bar

Of all the events, the high bar is the hardest on the hands. For this reason, gymnasts who do a lot of work on the bar often give their hands a rest by exercising on it only every other day. At the beginning stages, you won't be doing the kind of stunts that put the most stress on your skin. But even so, it's a good idea to stop exercising before your hands get too hot and start to blister.

There are a number of high bar grips, but we'll be using only three of them. These are the overgrip (the kind used for chin-ups), the undergrip (hands grab bar from beneath so that palms are toward you; the kind of grip used for pull-ups), and the mixed or combination grip in which one hand uses the overgrip and the other uses the undergrip.

To protect your hands, be sure to dust them with chalk before mounting the bar. Chalk up again whenever the previous coating wears off. You may also want to wear palm guards, though they won't be needed for most of the stunts in this chapter. And since caked chalk is especially hard on the hands, check to make sure the bar is completely clean and smooth. If it's not, go over it with a piece of emery paper or a very fine sandpaper.

Caring for Your Hands

Up to this point you haven't had to be concerned with your hands. But from now on you're going to be working on apparatus that can put a lot of stress on the skin of your palms and fingers. So it's important to know how to avoid problems and how to treat them when they occur.

The two main hand problems gymnasts run into are rips and blisters. They can be prevented by working the apparatus only until your hands get hot and a little red—and then stopping. That means that the first day or so you'll only be able to take a few swings on the high bar or do a few things on the other apparatus. But if you follow this procedure each day, your skin will gradually develop a protective layer of callus.

However, no matter how careful you are, at one time or another you'll probably get a rip or a tear in your hands. This problem sounds a lot worse than it really is. A rip or tear is just a shifting of a layer of skin that causes the top layer or two to peel off. It may hurt a little, but if you care for it properly, it will quickly heal and you'll be able to continue your training without a major interruption.

The best way to treat a rip is to tear or cut off the entire flap of skin over the open area. Use scissors sterilized by flame or with alcohol.

Then clean the area thoroughly as soon as possible with soap, water, and disinfectant. This will sting, but you've got to do it. Make sure the area is clean.

Apply some burn ointment or other medicated cream to kill the germs and the pain, and bandage the hand with gauze and tape. A rip heals best in the open air, so remove the bandage when you go to bed.

You should wear a bandage the first and possibly the second day after the rip when you're working out. This will keep the area from getting dirty. But after that you'll notice the new skin getting tougher. When this happens, be sure to use a lot of lotion, vaseline, or other high moisture cream to keep the new skin pliable. If it gets too dry and brittle, it will crack when you bend your hand, and you'll have to start all over again.

A rip will heal in three or four days. During that time, don't do any stunts that will put stress on the affected area. However, you can work on any apparatus that puts stress on other areas of your hand.

Once a rip has healed, begin to cautiously do the stunts that force you to use that area of your hand. Try to gradually build up a layer of callus on the new skin.

Blisters should be treated in much the same way. If the blister is near the surface, break it with a sterilized sewing needle, cut away the skin, and treat it like a rip. Be especially careful to keep it clean, as the small pocket a blister creates is an ideal breeding place for germs.

If the blister is deep within the skin, has not ruptured or torn, you've got no choice but to leave it alone and let the skin repair itself.

The Safe Way to Dismount

Set the bar high enough so that you can hang from it, arms fully extended overhead, without touching your feet to the floor. This is called the long hang position, and you should begin by jumping up and grasping the bar in an overgrip and then hanging to see how it feels.

When you're comfortable with the long hang, try a little swing. This will be fun, but don't let yourself get carried away. If you swing too vigorously, you may slip off the bar.

Now try a simple dismount. Sir Isaac Newton did a lot more than fool around with gravity and falling apples. He also discovered the principle that allows gymnasts to dismount safely. Sir Isaac found that there's no way a body going in one direction can go in the opposite direction unless the body stops first. On the high bar that means that before you can start to swing forward you've first got to stop swinging back (and vice versa). It's that stop or dead spot in your rear swing that you take advantage of to dismount safely.

Take a couple of swings on the bar and try to find that stop spot on your rear swing. Then swing a little more, find the spot, and release your hands. You'll drop to your feet for a controlled landing. Use this technique for getting off the bar from now on. *Don't try to dismount while you're swinging forward.* This is one of the most important safety rules when working the high bar.

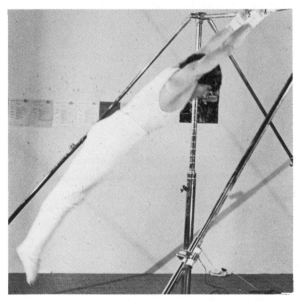

Try a little swing.

Then dismount at the stop spot
in your rearward swing.

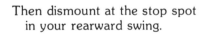

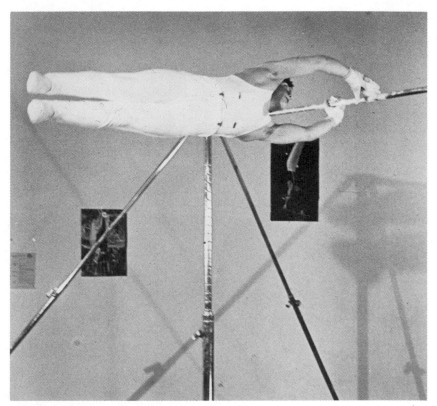

Pendulum swing with a half twist

Pendulum Swing with a Half Twist

Do a gentle swing so that your body passes only twenty to twenty-five degrees behind and in front of the vertical lines created by the bar supports. Then, at the peak of your forward swing, release your right hand and bring it around in front and to the left to regrasp the bar on the other side of your stationary hand. This will cause you to do a half twist.

You will now be facing the opposite direction as you swing like a pendulum. Your right hand will be in an overgrip and your left in an undergrip as a result of the twist. Swing with this mixed or combination grip once or twice and then dismount at the stop spot of your rear swing. Do the same stunt the other way, too, using your left hand to initiate the twist.

From Mixed Grip to Overgrip

Do the same swing and half twist as before so that you are in a mixed grip. Swing a few times and then, when you reach the stop spot of one of your rear swings, release your left hand from its undergrip and regrasp with an overgrip. Do this stunt both ways.

The mixed or combination grip. The right hand is in an overgrip and the left hand is in an undergrip. Notice the straps and buckles of the gymnast's palm guards.

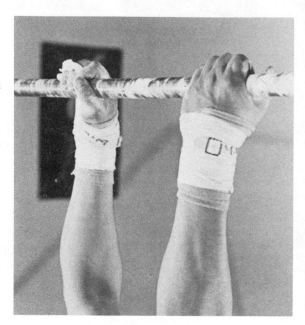

Skin-the-Cat

You will need someone to act as spotter for this stunt.

Begin by doing a long hang using an overgrip. Swing slightly and tuck your legs, bringing your knees up to your chest. Quickly put your tucked legs between your arms and balance in that upside-down tucked position for a moment.

Then straighten your legs toward the ceiling. Squeeze your knees up against your face and slowly—very slowly—lower your still-straight legs down behind you toward the floor. When your legs won't go any farther, release your hands and drop to the floor.

After you get used to this, do the same stunt without releasing your hands. Instead of dropping to the floor, pull your legs back up part way so that you are holding an inverted pike position. Then put them through your arms again, do a long hang, and drop to the mat. This is the complete skin-the-cat stunt.

b. Balance in an upside-down tuck for a moment.

a. Begin in a long hang.

SKIN-THE-CAT

c. Slowly lower your legs behind you to an inverted pike position.

d. Continue lowering your legs. . .

e. until they won't go any farther.
Then either dismount or return to
a long hang by doing everything
in reverse.

SINGLE KNEE SWING UP

a. Hook one knee over the bar.

b. Swing your front leg down as you pull yourself up.

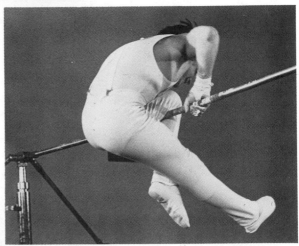

c. Then straighten your elbows and support yourself on your hands.

Single Knee Swing-Up

Begin from a long hang. Swing one leg up and pull it through your arms. Then hook it over the bar at the knee. Your other leg will simply remain out in front.

Now gently swing that front leg down and up a few times. Give one downswing a little extra speed. Use the momentum of that downswing to help you as you pull yourself up on top of the bar. Your hands will rotate upward.

Once you're on top, straighten your elbows and lift your hooked leg off the bar. You will now be supporting yourself on your hands and arms. One leg will be in front of the bar and one behind it. You'll be facing forward, one hand on either side of your body.

To dismount, lower yourself so that the same knee again hooks over the bar. Then just do everything in reverse order.

Learning on Low

Now that you have an idea of what the horizontal bar is like when at competition height, lower it to about chest level. The rest of the stunts in this chapter are a little more difficult, and you should master them completely on the low bar before trying them at a higher setting. In fact, you shouldn't try them at full height until both you and your instructor agree that you're ready.

The front support

Front Support

Jump up on the bar, grasping it with an overgrip so that your hands are on top of the bar. Support yourself solely on your arms. Swing slightly forward and back, keeping your body straight. On one of your rearward swings do a dismount, pushing off a little with your hands.

Pullover

Like the single knee swing up learned earlier, this is a way of getting your body up on top of the bar. Using an overgrip, step forward and plant one foot directly beneath the bar. At the same time, swing your other leg out and up in front. Try to swing this leg up so far that you almost touch your face. This will draw your waist in close to the bar.

Then quickly swing your stationary leg up to join the swing leg so that both are over the bar from the side opposite you and the bar is pressed tightly against your waist. The momentum created by your leg swings will force your legs over the bar and beyond. And, acting like a seesaw, your legs traveling down on the other side will pull your upper body under and up. You'll be turning around the bar on your waist.

With your body now on top, you'll find yourself in a front support position. Swing gently and dismount. Later, try a more advanced version of this trick by swinging both legs up from the floor at the same time.

THE PULLOVER

a. Plant one foot beneath the bar as you swing your other leg out and up.

b. Swing both legs so that the bar is pressed tightly against your waist. Your momentum will carry you around and into a front support.

Back Hip Circle

In this stunt, you swing all the way around the bar. In case you get stuck halfway or have some other difficulty, you should ask someone to spot for you.

Jump to a front support. Swing your legs forward and back slightly. On one of your forward swings, bend your elbows a little so that the bar is against your hips. At the same time, swing both legs forward and up, trying to bring them close to your face.

Press the bar hard against your hips and try to swing your legs fast enough to pull your body under and up, exactly as you did in the second part of the pullover. You should arrive again in the front support, having circled the bar completely.

The back hip circle: As your legs move downward they will pull the rest of your body up and into a front support.

Leg Cuts and Half Twist from Rear to Front Support

There is no quick and easy way to refer to this particular combination of moves. So, as is often the case in gymnastics, everybody's stuck with a long, descriptive name. As you'll see when you work the pommel horse, a leg cut is a move in which you bring your leg forward or to the rear, releasing your grip on the apparatus to allow the leg to pass and then regrasping the bar or pommel.

With a spotter to help you, begin this stunt in a front support. Then bring your right leg forward and over the bar, letting go with your right hand to allow the leg to pass and then quickly regrasping the bar. This is a right leg cut.

Next do a left leg cut.

You will now be in a rear support position, elbows straight, bar behind you. Release your left hand; turn it outward to the left; and regrasp the bar in an overgrip. Now you're ready for the half twist.

Let go with your right hand and twist to the left, pivoting on your left hand. Regrasp the bar with your right, and you'll be in a front support.

A word of caution here: As you twist, be careful not to roll your body along the bar. If you do, you may roll right over your left hand, and that can hurt. Instead, learn to use good form by shifting your weight quickly and doing the twist by sort of jumping around to the left.

LEG CUTS AND HALF TWIST TO FRONT SUPPORT

a. Cut your right leg forward.

b. From this position, do a left leg cut forward.

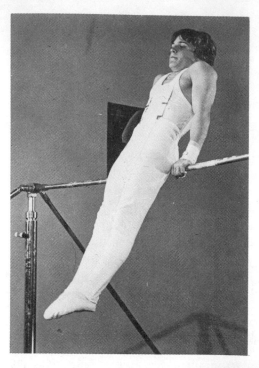

c. You'll now be in a rear support position.

d. Twist to the left, regrasping the bar with your right hand.

Flank Dismount

In this stunt, you more or less vault over the bar to one side and dismount. You should have a spotter to help you as you learn.

From a front support do a slight swing. As your body moves rearward on one of your swings, bring both legs back and up and then forward and over the bar on one side (left or right). As you release one hand to allow your legs to pass, you will cross over with your side to the bar. This will cause you to do a quarter twist to right or left. Once your body's over, release your stationary hand and drop to the mat. You'll be facing either to the right or left. Practice this stunt going over on each side.

The flank dismount

Underswing Dismount

As a first step in learning this skill, stand so that you can grasp the bar with your arms straight out in front of you. Do a little jump up off the floor and, picking your legs up, swing under the bar in either a pike or a tucked position. As you reach the stop spot of your forward swing, straighten your body and push the bar away overhead as you dismount.

Practice this for a while, gradually working up to the next step. For that next step, try jumping higher when you start the stunt. Then bring

THE UNDERSWING DISMOUNT

a. Swing under the bar in pike position.

b. At the stop spot of your swing, straighten out the pike. . .

your knees or thighs up near the bar while keeping your legs straight. You will be swinging under the bar in pike position, head lower than your hips.

When you reach the stop spot of your forward swing, straighten out the pike and vigorously push the bar away overhead as you fly into your landing. As you gain more confidence, try for more height with your legs and more distance on the flight following your release. Once you get really good at this, you can add a half twist during your flight so that you land facing back the way you came.

c. and push the bar away overhead. . .

d. as you fly into your landing.

Underswing Dismount from a Front Support

You should probably have a spotter as you learn this stunt.

From a front support position, lift your legs forward and upward. At the same time, lean back with your shoulders, keeping the bar against your thighs. Your legs will be coming up as your shoulders are going down.

Keep going until your legs are almost vertical, toes pointed at the ceiling. You will be in the pike position you passed through when doing the underswing dismount. And you continue just as in that stunt. Push your legs away from the bar; straighten your body; push the bar away overhead, and fly to a landing.

If you've already mastered the underswing dismount, this stunt should be no problem. But do be careful not to try helping things along by swinging when in the front support position. If you do, you may lose your grip when you get underneath the bar. Instead, practice lifting your legs gently and leaning back gently with your shoulders.

Suggested Low Bar Routine

It may be a while before you're ready to try these stunts on the high bar. In the meantime, you might want to try a short routine on the low bar in order to work on smooth transitions from one stunt to another. You probably shouldn't try this until you can do the stunts fairly well, but once you're moderately proficient, there's no reason why you can't mix the stunts to create a short routine of your own. Here's just one suggestion:

1. Pullover
2. Back hip circle
3. Right leg cut
4. Left leg cut (you will now be in a rear support)
5. Half twist from rear support back to front support
6. Underswing dismount

7
The Rings

Before 1962, gymnastic competition in the United States included two ring events: the flying rings and the still rings. The flying rings event required a gymnast to do stunts and tricks while swinging back and forth like a trapeze performer. Because some stunts involved letting go of the rings and regrasping them in mid air, the rings had to be heavy so they wouldn't go flying away out of reach when the gymnast released them. Consequently, they were usually made of steel coated with rubber.

You can still find flying rings in many gyms today, but the event is no longer performed in competition. The flying rings were dropped primarily because, like the rope climb, it was strictly an American event, and gymnastics coaches felt that the U.S. program should include only the events that are a part of international competition.

So today gymnasts concentrate on the still rings. Still rings have an inside diameter of seven inches and are usually made of laminated wood, making them much lighter than the flying rings. They are hung so that they are 19 5/8 inches apart and 8 1/2 feet above the floor. They may be hung from cables attached to the ceiling beams of a gym, or from a special ring frame which uses floor sockets and guy wires for support.

The height of the rings, like that of the horizontal bar, should be adjustable. So when you're scouting out prospective gyms, check to see whether the rings can be raised and lowered. Some gyms may have two sets of rings, one set at the competition height and the other about four feet off the ground. Or a gym may use a big table covered with a six-by-twelve or eight-by-twelve floor mat. The table is used to raise the performer to the rings instead of doing it the other way around.

And speaking of mats, you should have a stack of at least two four-inch competition mats beneath you and preferably an eight-inch soft foam mat on top of that. Since we won't be doing any swinging dismounts at this level, twelve-foot-long mats are sufficient. Center the mat stack under the rings, of course.

Strength is the central element of almost all ring work, so you may not be able to perform these stunts the first time you try them. If you can't, don't get discouraged. As you continue to try, you'll be amazed at how well your body will respond and at how quickly your strength builds. Be sure to chalk up before getting on the rings, and be sure to have a spotter or your instructor standing by whenever indicated. Until you get used to the rings, in fact, it's a good idea to have your instructor nearby for all stunts, and definitely for all those done on the high rings.

High Rings

Learning to Hang and Swing

Let's start out on the high rings (competition height) so you can get a feel for the apparatus. Jump up or have someone lift you to the rings and just hang there with your arms above your head.

Now try to swing back and forth a little. As on the high bar, don't get carried away with your swing. A swing of twenty to twenty-five degrees on either side of the vertical is plenty.

At first it's okay to swing any way you like. But you should quickly learn to keep your arms straight. Do not bend your elbows. Also, try to swing from your shoulders with your body held fairly straight. You may bend a little at the waist when going forward and arch your back a bit going rearward, but that's all.

This won't be easy. But it's important to learn the correct swing from Day One, for learning to do it properly now will pay off years later. If you don't master it from the start, you'll get into some bad habits that will be extremely difficult to break later on.

I think one of the best ways to learn this technique is to picture your body from hands to toes as a straight stick. Then pretend that there is a pin stuck through the middle of the stick (your waist). Everything turns around this pin. If your legs swing backward, your top half must swing forward, for example. It also helps if you try to keep your shoulders straight and try to push the rings forward when your feet go backward and vice versa.

LEARNING THE PROPER SWING

a. Picture your body as a stick. . .

b. with everything turning around a pin stuck in its middle.

Inverted Pike

This stunt is a lot easier to describe than it is to do, but with a little strength in the right places it shouldn't be too difficult. Jump up into the hang position and swing your legs up and through your arms. Then slowly continue moving your legs backward until they are horizontal or, in other words, parallel to the floor. Your eyes should be looking up at the support cables and your head should remain squarely on your shoulders.

Balance in this inverted pike for several seconds. Then, holding the pike as tightly as you can with your knees close to your face, lower your legs slowly behind you. When your legs reach their limit, simply let go of the rings and drop down to your feet.

The inverted pike

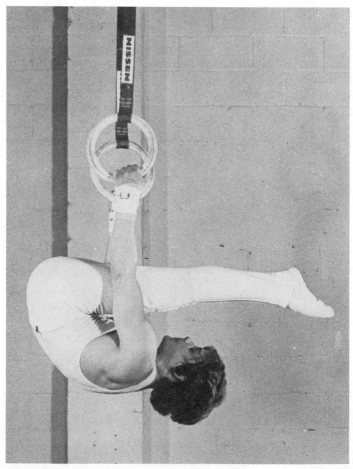

Skin-the-Cat

Do the same stunt described above, only this time don't drop off. When your legs reach their limit as you move them behind you, stop and slowly bring them back up to the inverted pike.

The next step is to lower yourself to a hang, but you've got to do it very slowly. Using all the muscle power you can, bring your legs forward out of the pike and lower them in front of you. Don't give up midway and let them fall down by themselves. They could easily fall with enough force to pull you off the rings. If you find that you can't make it, ask your instructor to grab your legs and help you. When your legs are down and you're back in the hang, hold the position for a moment until you're stable. Then drop to the floor. The stunt will look very much like a skin-the-cat on the horizontal bar, except, of course, you'll be holding onto the rings instead of the bar.

As you've probably noticed, it takes a lot of strength to do a skin-the-cat slowly. And while there are some stunts in which you can swing into or out of a position, the stunt you've just completed is more typical of the kind of exercise a gymnast does on the rings.

Hanging Half Lever

This skill calls for another demonstration of muscle power, particularly in the stomach. From a hang, with arms straight, bring your legs up to a horizontal position in front of you. If you can raise your legs at all, you're doing really well. And if you can hold them absolutely horizontal for three seconds, you've got a major accomplishment to your credit.

The hanging half lever

The chances are, however, that you won't be able to do this stunt the first, second, or even third time you try it. You'll probably have to build up your stomach muscles first. And the best way to do that is to simply try the stunt every day until your muscles are strong enough.

Straight Body Inverted Hang

You definitely need the instructor for this stunt.

Begin from a hang. Do a gentle swing, and on one of your forward motions raise your legs into an inverted pike. Balance there for a moment and then very slowly straighten your body in an upside-down position.

STRAIGHT BODY
INVERTED HANG

a. From an inverted pike,
   slowly bring your legs up
   between the cables.

Push your legs up between the cables, continuing to watch your feet as you do so. Try to force your body into a straight line between the cables. If your muscles aren't used to the demands you are making upon them, you may find that your arms are shaking a bit. You can counteract this by squeezing your arms tightly against your sides.

Once you're steady, move your head back until you can look at the floor beneath you. You'll have to concentrate on where your feet are to keep them from leaving the correct position.

To return to an upright hang, reverse the sequence. Look back up at your feet and slowly lower your legs to an inverted pike. Then lower yourself—slowly—to a hang.

b. Keep your eyes on your feet until you're steady. Then move your head back so that you can see the floor beneath you.

Working the Low Rings

From this point on, the rings should be set at about chest height.

Basic Support Position

Grasp the rings so that your arms are next to the cables and your hands are inside the rings holding on to the top of the lower half of each ring. You will be using your arms to support yourself and you may want to bend your elbows at first. Once you're steady, though, try to straighten your arms and bring your body to "Attention" with chest up, back straight, head up, etc. Then hold that position so that you're steady. This support position takes some strength, but it may help to squeeze the rings tightly against your sides at this point.

This stunt doesn't require any complicated moves, but you've got to be extremely careful when mounting the rings. As you get on, do not let the rings get out to the side. Squeeze them against your legs. Also, don't let them get even an inch behind you. If that happens, you may fall forward. But if you make a mistake and do fall forward, be absolutely

The basic support position

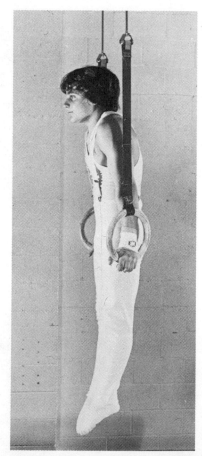

certain to let go of the rings *immediately.* If you hold on as you fall, you can damage your shoulder and arm muscles.

To come down from the support, quickly push your hands and the rings out to the side. Let go. And jump down to your feet.

The Support L

This stunt gets its name from the L shape your body takes as you perform it. Begin in the basic support position and, keeping your knees straight, raise your legs up in front of you until they're horizontal and parallel with the floor. Hold this position for three seconds and lower to the support. Dismount.

The L requires the same stomach strength as the half lever. But, as you'll discover, doing it in the support position makes it much more difficult. Yet, believe it or not, the support L is considered a rest position in advanced gymnastics. Eventually you'll develop so much strength that you'll look forward to being able to take a breather in a routine by doing a support L.

The support L

Tuck Shoulder Balance and Shoulder Stand

This trick requires quite a bit of strength. And when you're learning it, it also requires the presence of your instructor.

Begin by going into the support L. Then bend your knees and draw yourself into a tuck. Tilt forward, bringing your seat and feet up behind. Continue tilting until you can bend your arms so that your shoulders will be between the rings. Your hips and feet will be up over your head and you will be in an inverted tuck position, head down, eyes on the floor. Someone should be standing by to spot for you.

If you can, balance in this position for a moment. Then straighten your legs so that your body is up between the cables. You should be holding on with only your hands. This position is called a shoulder stand.

To get down, perform all of these operations in reverse order. Bring your legs down into a tuck. Tilt backward until you're back in the support position and either return to the L or gently lower your legs beneath you and dismount.

Tuck shoulder balance

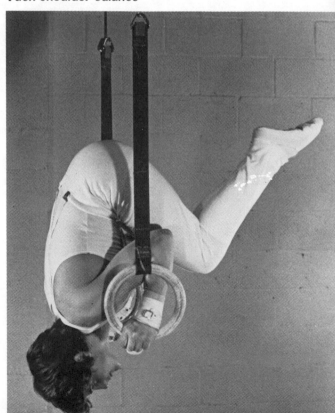

Eliminating the Curl and Building Strength

In both the support and the shoulder stand, you'll have a tendency to pull the rings in and curl them toward your body. You may also be inclined to lean against the cables. This is something you should try to avoid.

Instead, think of the bottom part of the rings as two stationary parallel bars that cannot be twisted or moved. Try to support yourself just as you would if this were really the case.

Also, as you become more proficient, work at doing the stunts described in this chapter without pressing the rings into your body. It's okay to do it when you're learning, but in competition the only parts of your body allowed to touch the rings are your hands. Judges will take off points if they see you leaning against the cables or curling the rings into your body.

As far as building your strength, the best thing is to simply work the rings. Some gymnasts get into weight lifting, but it really isn't necessary. By trying the stunts repeatedly until you can do them, you'll be building precisely the muscles you'll need.

Suggested Rings Routine

Once you've learned the basics of the stunts presented in this chapter, you can practice most of them on your own. And after you can do each of them individually, you might want to link them together to create a short routine. Often you'll find that the final position of one skill leads naturally into the beginning position of another, making it easy to link the two.

The miniroutine given here shows one way the stunts in this chapter might be arranged, but as you become more proficient, you're sure to think of many others.

1. Jump up to a hang position. Take a moment to steady yourself so that you can begin from a perfectly still position.
2. Swing your legs up and do an inverted pike.
3. Hold the final inverted pike position, legs horizontal, for a moment. Then continue lowering your legs to a skin-the-cat position.
4. Come up out of the skin-the-cat position and lower to a hang.
5. Swing up to a straight body inverted hang.
6. Lower yourself to the basic support position.
7. Do a support L.
8. Tilt forward and do a tuck shoulder balance.

9. Hold that position for a moment and then straighten into a shoulder stand.

10. Lower yourself to a hanging half lever position.

11. Hold it a moment and then lower to a hang.

12. Dismount.

8
The Parallel Bars

The parallel bars are a comparatively recent invention. Introduced in Germany in the mid-nineteenth century by Frederick Jahn, they are probably the one piece of apparatus that has no counterpart outside the gym. The horizontal bar may have been derived from a tree limb and the pommel horse from a live horse and saddle, but the parallel bars were created specifically for gymnastics.

The rails of the bars are oval-shaped with an average thickness of two inches. In years past, they were made of very stiff wood. But recently wood has been replaced by fiberglass. Fiberglass bars are produced with a surface texture resembling wood, but they are much more flexible and springy. This makes them more comfortable to work on and it allows the gymnast to develop more height on some stunts.

Each rail is eleven and one-half feet long, and each is attached to vertical supports at either end. The supports are adjustable, making it possible to raise or lower (from four feet to five and one-half feet) the bars to suit your height and to change the distance between the bars from sixteen and one-half to nineteen inches. Learning how to adjust the bars should be the very first thing you learn on this apparatus. Different manufacturers use different systems, so it's important to ask someone how it's done before attempting it yourself.

When raising or lowering the bars, be sure to always have someone help you. With each of you supporting one end of the bar and releasing the adjusting mechanism, you'll have no problem. However, if you try it alone, the bar could drop quickly and hit you on the head. Also, never hold onto the metal pole attached to the bar when you're adjusting the height. That pole slides into the base section, and there's always a chance that you'll get your fingers pinched. Instead, hold on to the bar with one hand and release the adjusting mechanism with the other.

In competition, each performer may adjust the apparatus to suit himself, and most set the bars at about eye level. However, for learning you should set it at about stomach or low chest height. This will make mounting and dismounting easier, and you'll have less distance to fall if you make a mistake. The width of the bars should be adjusted so that you can stand between them and are able to jump straight up with your arms at your sides. The bars should be about half an inch from either shoulder.

Mats should extend five to six feet on either side of the bars, and the metal base should be completely covered. Some gyms use custom-fitted mats especially designed for the parallel bars, but properly placed standard mats will do as well. The important thing is that no metal be left exposed. You should see only the bars and the uprights. When learning, you ought to have at least four inches of mat protection. Eight inches would be even better.

The rules say that a parallel bars routine must consist of swinging, flight, and hold exercises which may also involve a certain amount of strength work. Swinging usually means holding onto the bars with your hands while moving your body in between them. Often you'll swing from one stunt into the next. Flight involves losing contact with the bars completely and at advanced levels can include saltos and twists. Hold exercises are balance positions like a handstand, and strength work would include things like pressing to a handstand.

In this chapter, we'll learn stunts that require one or more of each of these elements and then see how to link them together in a routine. The bars should be set at stomach or low chest level while learning most of these skills, and you should be sure to have an instructor or spotter present where indicated.

The Basic Support Position

Mount the apparatus by jumping up and supporting yourself with your two hands. Your arms should be straight, as should your legs (toes pointed) and the rest of your body. This is the basic support position for the parallel bars.

The L Support

As on the rings, the L support is a strength trick, letting you show the world the power of your stomach muscles. From the basic support, see if you can raise your legs until they are horizontal. Your body should form an L and you should try to hold the position for two or three seconds.

This sounds easy, but you may not be able to do it right away. If you can't, keep trying until your stomach muscles have developed further. If you try the L several times each day that you are in the gym, this won't take long.

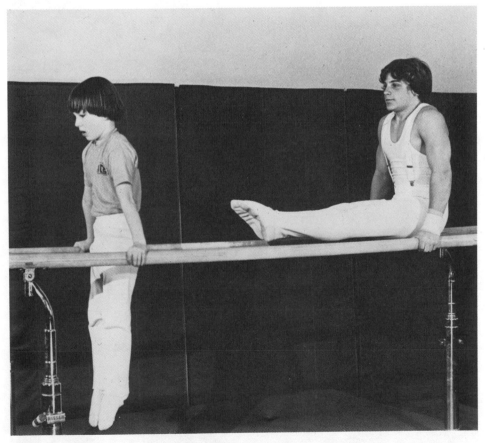

The basic support position (left) and the support L (right)

Walking on the Bars

Walking on the bars with your hands is similar to walking on the ground with your feet. Both skills involve shifting your weight while moving forward one step at a time.

Begin in the support position with your muscles fairly rigid. Right from the beginning you should practice concentrating on all of the parts of your body simultaneously—toes pointed, knees straight, legs rigid, arms straight, head looking straight ahead, etc.

a.

WALKING ON THE BARS

a. Notice how the gymnast shifts. . .
b. his weight and takes small. . .
c. steps with his hands.

Start to walk by shifting your weight to the right and moving your left hand forward a few inches. Then shift to the left and move your right hand. Keep repeating this sequence until you reach the end of the bars.

Be sure to take only very small steps. Each hand should move forward just a few inches at a time. Otherwise you won't be able to shift your weight properly. Also, concentrate on going slowly. If you go too fast, you'll have trouble controlling the momentum created by your weight shifts.

b.   c.

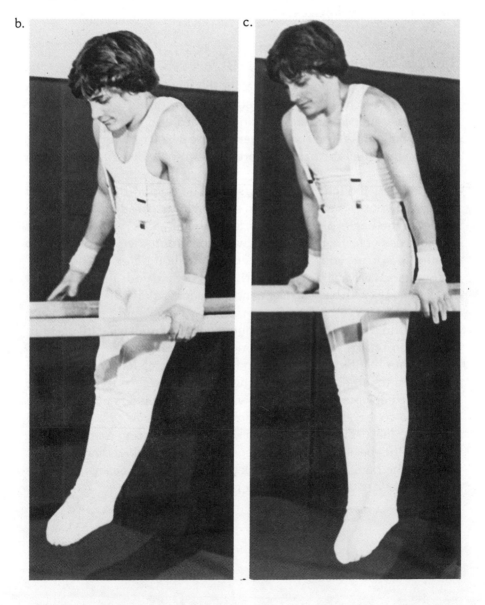

Swinging

Since swinging is such an important part of the parallel bars event, it's a good idea to begin mastering the technique immediately. You begin in the support position and start your body moving forward and back in a gentle swing similar to a pendulum. Your arms remain rigid and straight as your body swings from your shoulders.

This is a lot of fun, but it's easy to go too fast, lose control, and fall through the bars. Your feet should not rise above the bars in either direction at this point.

Straddle-Sit

This is a rest position which takes the weight off your arms for a moment or two. It's also a basic starting position for many stunts.

From the support position, swing forward and back two or three times to build up a little speed. Then on one swing forward, bring your feet up higher than the bars and spread them so that you've got a leg on each rail.

Remember, though, your body should be rigid in the support and swing, and your legs should remain straight in the straddle. You will be sitting on the backs of your thighs, legs straight, toes pointed. The bar should cross your thigh about midway from your knee to your hip, so be sure to spread your legs wide enough as you enter the position.

Your hands will still be grasping the bars behind you, and you should be "sitting tall" with back straight and shoulders square. If your position is good and you're balanced, try releasing your hands and bringing them around to grasp the bar in front of you as if preparing for another trick. Then return them to their original position.

With your hands on the bar behind you, quickly pick up your legs and bring them together. Then swing them down to return to the support position. Keep your downswing slow and as controlled as possible. You may have to bend your knees slightly to do this at first. But you'll eventually learn the trick of lifting your legs by sitting a little deeper between the bars. When your legs are straight, lowering yourself between the bars acts to lever the legs upward like a seesaw. And that takes less effort than doing it with pure muscle power.

SWING TO A STRADDLE-SIT

a. From a basic support position. . .

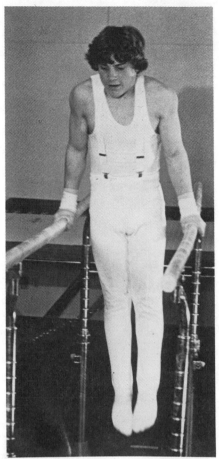

b. swing your legs forward, and spread them as they rise above the bars.

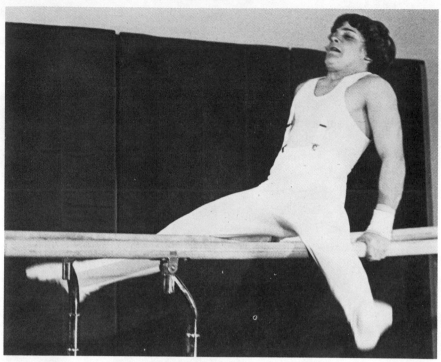

c. Land in a straddle-sit with your thighs on the bars.

d. When your position is good, try bringing your hands around to grasp the bars in front of you.

Upper Arm Hang

You'll have to raise the bars to shoulder level before trying this one. And you should wear a long-sleeved sweat shirt to protect the skin on your upper arm.

Stand between the bars. Reach up and over the bars and, bending your elbows and putting them out to either side, grasp the bars about one foot in front of your shoulders. Then bend your knees and pick up your feet.

You will be in a shoulder hang with most of your weight hanging from your upper arms. This is another basic position, and many tricks can be begun from it. However, with all that weight on your arms, it may be a little uncomfortable. You can make it easier by keeping your elbows level with the bars and by tightening all of your arm muscles to create a kind of cushion between the bar and the bone.

The upper arm hang

Swing from an Upper Arm Hang

Now raise the bars to about eye level or high enough for your toes to clear the floor when you are in an upper arm hang.

Jump up to an upper arm hang as before. This time, though, your body should be straight with toes pointed. In fact, try to get your muscles to automatically straighten your legs and point your toes when you work the parallel bars. Nearly every trick on the bars requires your legs to be straight from hip to toe. So it's important to make straight legs a habit as soon as possible.

From the upper arm hang you can begin swinging back and forth, but remember to keep it gentle and controlled. Swing several times and then take a rest by bringing your legs up and looping them over the bars, bending your knees. Then straighten your legs and slowly lower them back to the upper arm hang and swing some more.

Swing from Upper Arm Hang to Straddle-Sit

Here's a trick you'll use quite often. With the bars at eye level, jump up to an upper arm hang. Start to swing, and as you come forward on one of your swings, bring your legs up and over the bar as if you were going into the rest position learned previously. Only this time, don't bend your knees. Keep your legs straight and straighten your arms as you raise your body to a straddle-sit.

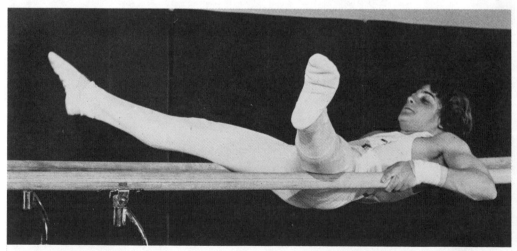

Swing from an upper arm hang to this position. Then straighten your arms to rise to a straddle-sit.

Forward Shoulder Roll

For this stunt and for those that follow, the bars should be set at stomach or low chest level. Also, you'll need someone to spot for you as you're learning this one.

Start in the support position and swing up to a straddle-sit. When you're sitting tall and on balance, bring your hands forward to grasp the bar in front of your legs. Bend forward, putting your elbows out to the side as far as they'll go. Keep bending until you place your upper arms on the bars, making contact at a point near your shoulders.

Now pull your hips up and over your head so that your legs come off the bar. You'll be doing a sort of forward roll on the bar with your legs in straddle position. Keep your legs apart as you roll forward, elbows out to the sides. The idea is to roll across the top of the bar.

As your legs come off the bars and rise above you, you'll be in something like an upside-down upper arm hang with your weight supported on your upper arms near the shoulders. At this point, release your hands and, as your body moves down and forward, regrasp them as you would for a regular upper arm hang.

Your body will roll forward and, since your legs have remained apart, you will arrive in the same position you would use to rise from an upper arm hang to a straddle-sit. And that's exactly what you should do to complete the stunt.

THE FORWARD SHOULDER ROLL
a. From a straddle-sit, bend forward to put your upper arms on the bars.

b. Pull your hips up and over your head so that your legs come off the bars.

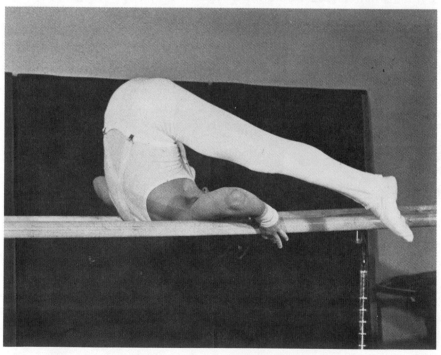

c. You'll be in something like an upside-down upper arm hang. Next, release your hands and roll forward, keeping your legs apart.

Shoulder Stand or Shoulder Balance

You'll need your instructor or someone else who can spot for you when learning this one.

Swing from a support to a straddle-sit. Bring your hands around to grasp the bars in front of you. Lean forward, keeping your elbows as far out to the sides as you can. Make contact with the rails on your upper arms near your shoulders.

Now you can bend your knees and place one foot on each bar. Keep bending forward until the top part of your body is upside down. Once balanced in this position, take your legs off the bar and join them so that you're in something of an upside down L.

If you feel secure at this point, slowly raise your legs until they are straight above you. Going slowly is important so you don't lose your balance. Ask the spotter to help you raise your legs if necessary.

You will now be in a shoulder stand. You can come down out of it by lowering your legs back onto the bars and reversing the sequence. Or you can carefully lower your joined legs down past the bars so that you arrive in an upper arm hang.

As you become better at this trick, try to perform it without placing your feet on the bars before raising your legs. And, of course, practice to make the whole thing seem like a single, flowing motion.

The shoulder stand: To complete the stunt, the gymnast will bring his legs together to create an upside-down L support.

Rear Dismount

Here's a good way to end a routine. Once you're confident of your swing from a support, swing your legs forward until they are above the bars. You will be in a pike position.

At that moment begin to swing your whole body to the right, releasing your left hand and using it to help push your body in that direction. When your seat has cleared the right bar and you're headed down toward the mat, release your right hand as well. A split second later, grasp the bar with your left hand and land. The left hand will help you control your landing. You'll be facing your original direction with your left side to the apparatus.

You can also do a rear dismount to the left, and you should practice doing it both ways.

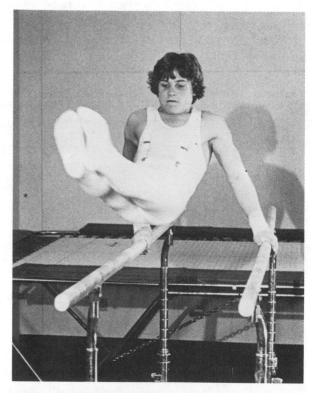

THE REAR DISMOUNT
a. Swing your whole body to the right.

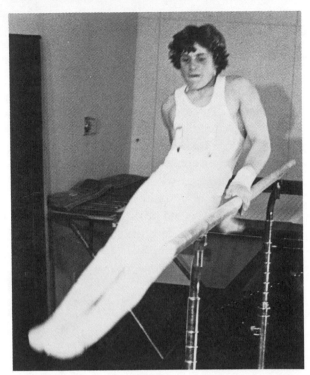

b. Release your right hand and grasp
   the bar with your left.

c. Use your left hand and arm to help
   control your landing.

Front Vault Dismount

Don't attempt this one until you have thoroughly mastered the skill of swinging. Begin in a support and start to swing. Try to swing forward with enough speed to get a good backswing—one powerful enough to bring your legs up behind the bars. When your body is at the peak of its backswing, vigorously push off the left bar and start your body moving over the right bar.

As the front of your body passes the right bar, release your right hand and grab the bar with your left. Drop to the mat with your left hand holding the bar and controlling the landing. Practice this dismount going to both sides.

**THE FRONT VAULT
DISMOUNT**

a. At the peak of the backswing,
   push off the left bar.

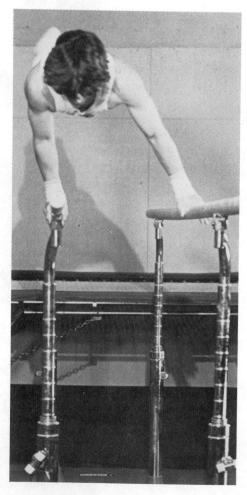

b. Grasp the bar with your left hand as you release your right. . .

c. and head toward a landing.

Straddle Travel

Like walking on your hands, this is a way to move your body along the bar. Begin from a straddle-sit, hands behind you. Bring your hands forward and grasp the bars in front, about a foot ahead of your thighs.

Lean forward and support your weight on your hands. As you're leaning, take your legs off the bars behind you, bring them together, and swing them forward and up into the straddle position again.

Repeating this sequence several times in a row will bring you to the other end of the bars. When you get there, simply get off and on again and travel to the opposite end.

Rear Swing and Scissors to Straddle-Sit

This is a key stunt because it allows you to change direction during a routine and head back the way you came. It's probably the most challenging parallel bars stunt we've done, and you should definitely have a spotter when you're learning it.

Begin in a straight arm support position and start to swing. Build up enough speed to bring your legs up above the bars at the peak of your rear swing. This will bring your body into a position nearly horizontal and parallel to the bars. At that point scissor your legs as you do a half twist to the left or right.

Let's assume you're twisting to the right. Your legs will scissor so that your right leg comes over onto the left bar and your left leg comes up onto the right bar. At the same time, you will be pushing off with your right hand to help you do a half twist to the right. You then release your left hand and bring it under and up to grasp what used to be the right bar, while your right hand comes over and grasps what used to be the left bar.

You will arrive in a straddle-sit, but you'll be facing the opposite direction.

Rear swing scissors (twisting to the right): The left leg comes under and the right leg goes over.

Suggested Parallel Bars Routine

When you've mastered the stunts in this chapter, try linking them together into a short routine. You can use the following routine to practice the stunts themselves, to practice making smooth transitions, and possibly even in competition. The bars should be set at eye level.

1. Jump to an upper arm hang.
2. Swing forward and bring your legs over the bars in a straddle.
3. Push yourself up so that your arms are straight. You will now be in a straddle-sit.
4. Reach forward to grasp the bars and swing to another straddle (straddle travel).
5. From the straddle-sit, rejoin your legs and swing forward in the support position.
6. On your rearward swing, scissor your legs to a straddle-sit, doing a half twist so that you end facing the opposite direction.
7. Place your hands on the bars in front of you and lean forward to perform a shoulder balance.
8. Lower your legs from the shoulder balance and swing forward to a straddle-sit, releasing your hands and grasping the bars behind you.
9. From this straddle-sit, quickly join your legs in front and swing rearward for a front vault dismount.

9
The Pommel Horse

The pommel horse, or side horse, has a fascinating history. It evolved from the wooden horse and saddle first used to train soldiers in the Roman cavalry. Centuries later knights in the Middle Ages used a modified version of the same apparatus to solve some problems of their own. As you can imagine, it's hard enough to just walk around in a full suit of armor, let alone to try getting on a horse.

So for the medieval knight, mounting his fiery charger could be something of a challenge. And possibly out of consideration for their faithful beasts, knights used to practice getting on and off four-legged wooden horses. Because of the terrific weight they had to hoist, knights would grip the high front and rear edges of the saddle to pull themselves up. These edges later became the U-shaped handles or pommels of today's side horse.

The wooden horse was eventually stuffed and covered with leather for use in gymnastics. But it was a long time before the outline of the original horse shape completely disappeared. Even today, in some older gyms, you may occasionally find a pommel horse with four legs and a "neck" that goes up at one end and a rounded "rump" at the other end.

The modern pommel horse is a two-legged affair with a body that is 63 to 64 inches long and about 14 inches across the top. The height is adjustable, but international regulations require a height of 43 5/16 inches in competition. In America, the horse may be set at 45 1/2 inches for taller gymnasts.

The pommels are made of wood and are also adjustable. They are 4 3/4 inches high and by moving them to the left or right, the distance between them can be set anywhere from 15 3/4 to 17 3/4 inches. Almost all stunts on the side horse involve grasping one or both of the pommels and using them to support the rest of your body. In competition, you are required to use all three parts of the horse (the center and both ends), and you must support your weight exclusively on your hands and arms. This is one of the reasons why the side horse is usually considered the most difficult event in gymnastics.

Preparing the Horse

The height of the horse isn't too important when you are just starting out. The only time it will make any difference to you is when you are getting on. So to make mounting easier, you may want to lower the horse to about waist level.

As far as the pommels go, there's no real rule on adjusting their width. Because of your size you may want to have them relatively close together. But remember that by moving them closer you increase the distance from each pommel to the end of the horse nearest to it. This can be an important consideration because at times you'll be supporting yourself with one hand on one pommel and the other hand on the end of the horse.

Be sure to arrange several four-inch-thick mats so that they surround the horse.

The Basic Idea

The main principle of all side horse work is really rather simple. Basically you support yourself on one or both hands and swing one or both legs either forward or backward to the left or to the right. However, within this general framework, the variety of stunts you can do is almost infinite.

One of the most important of these is the "cut." A cut refers to the action of moving your leg (or legs) from one side of the horse to the other while momentarily releasing one hand to let it pass. When your leg has cleared, you then regrasp the pommel or the end of the horse. As you'll discover, there are both single and double leg cuts, cuts forward and cuts to the rear, etc.

Single Leg Cut Mount to Straddle Support

To mount the horse for the first time, grasp both pommels and swing up into the "saddle." You'll have to release one hand to allow your body to pass, and you'll end up sitting between the pommels facing one end of the horse.

Dismount and do the same thing, only this time do not sit down and do not turn your body to face the end of the horse. Grasp both pommels and swing your leg (we'll assume it's your right leg) up over the right pommel, releasing and regrasping the pommel with your right hand. You should finish facing your original direction with one leg on each side of the horse. This is called a straddle support.

It's important to emphasize at this point that you should also be supporting yourself with only your hands. You've got to hold yourself up so that your legs carry no weight at all. Actually, they shouldn't even be touching the horse. This is true of many stunts done on this apparatus.

So keep your arms straight, your spine straight, and your shoulders back so you "sit tall," and your legs straight with toes pointed. This is a difficult position to assume the first few times, but it's basic to the side horse and should be practiced and learned thoroughly.

SINGLE LEG CUT MOUNT TO STRADDLE SUPPORT

a. Cut your right leg forward as you release. . .

b. and regrasp the pommel with your right hand.

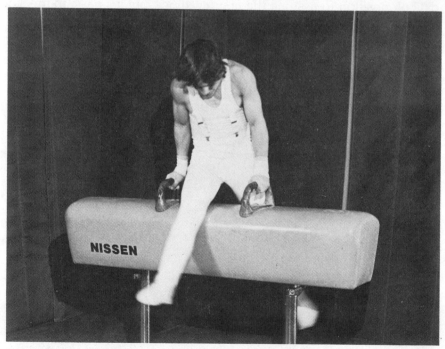

c. You'll arrive in a straddle support.

Single Leg Cut Forward to a Rear Support

Now you're ready for your first stunt on the horse. Do a single leg cut mount so that you finish in a straddle support with your left leg forward and right leg to the rear. (You can and should do all of these stunts with your legs in reverse position.)

From your straddle position bring your right leg around to the front. That is, cut your right leg forward, releasing and regrasping the pommel with your right hand. You will now be in a rear support position (so-called because the rear of your body is closest to the horse) with both hands on the pommels behind you.

In the rear support, try to keep your body as straight as possible. Of course, you won't be able to make your body perfectly vertical. The backs of your thighs are allowed to lightly touch the horse, but they should not support any weight and you should not bend at the hips.

The rear support

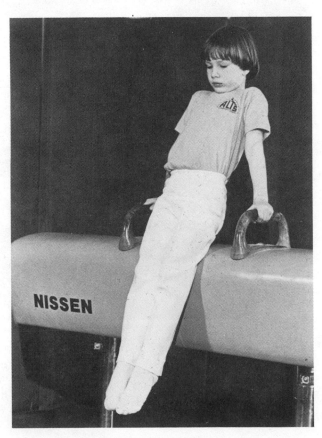

Two Rear Leg Cuts to a Front Support

Beginning in the rear support position, cut your left leg to the rear so that you are in a straddle, right leg in front, left leg behind. Then cut your right leg to the rear as well.

This leaves you in a front support. And again, your body should be as straight as possible. The front of your thighs may touch the horse, but they shouldn't support any weight.

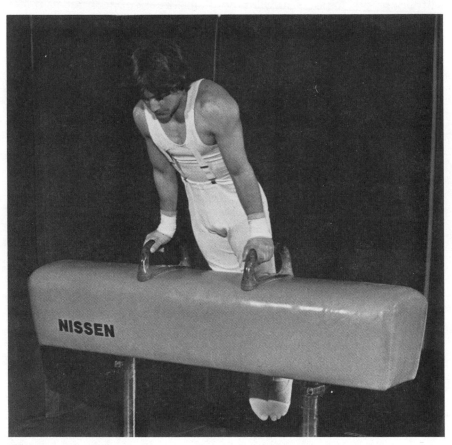

The front support

Weight Shifting and Rhythm

By now you've probably begun to realize how important it is to shift your weight when doing leg cuts. Weight shifting is a basic skill for all horse work, and it's something you should always be aware of.

Repeat the leg cuts described above, only this time emphasize your weight shifts as much as possible. For example, from a straddle support, left leg forward, do a leg cut to the rear to a front support. As you bring your left leg back, lean way over onto the right pommel and try to get your body up and away from the horse. Then as your left hand regrasps the left pommel, shift your weight back so that it's evenly distributed over both hands. Practice cutting both legs in both directions until shifting your weight becomes a natural part of the exercise.

Rhythm is also an essential element of side horse work, particularly because the rules require "clean swings without stops." As you may have noticed, when you're in a rear support, swinging your front leg to the rear can be touch to do. Shifting your weight makes it easier, but doing it with rhythm makes it easier still.

To see what I mean, try this experiment. Get into a straddle support, left leg forward. Now cut your right leg forward as if you were going to do a rear support. However, as your right leg arrives in its forward position, immediately shift your weight onto the right pommel and allow your right leg to "knock" your left leg into a cut to the rear. You'll finish in a straddle support, right leg forward.

The key to this exercise is using the right leg to get the left leg started. The right leg acts like a billiard ball or a croquet ball and transfers some of its motion to the left leg, making it much easier to do the rear leg cut.

Next, cut your right leg to the rear and use it to knock your left leg into a forward leg cut. Then cut your right leg forward and knock the left leg backward again.

Try to develop a four-count rhythm as you do these leg cuts. Begin in a front support. One: left leg cuts forward to a straddle support. Two: right leg cuts forward to knock left leg. Three: left leg cuts back to another straddle support. Four: right leg cuts backward to knock left leg. And so on.

As you get better at it, you can increase your speed. Pretty soon you'll find that you're *swinging* your legs instead of lifting them. Practice these leg cuts by doing four or five repetitions of the four-count without stopping.

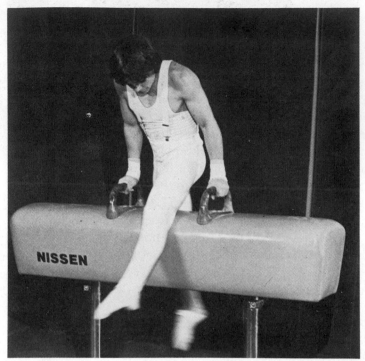

a. Count one: Left leg cuts forward to a straddle support.

WEIGHT SHIFTING AND RHYTHM

b. Count two: Right leg cuts forward to knock left leg back. After shifting your weight onto the left pommel to cut your right leg forward, you have to shift it onto the right pommel to knock the left leg back.

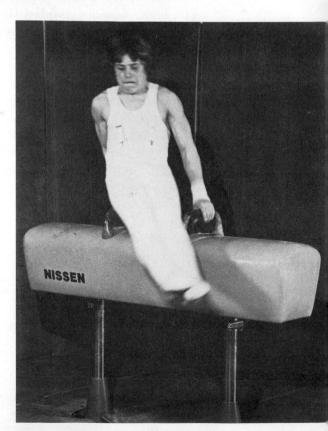

c. Count three: Left leg cuts back to another straddle support. Weight is on right pommel.

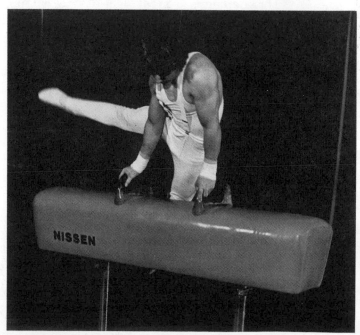

d. Count four: Right leg cuts back. Weight has been shifted to left pommel.

Half Double Leg Circle, Forward and Rearward

For this trick you use the same skills of weight shifting and rhythm learned for the four-count leg cuts. Only this time, instead of your right leg knocking your left into a forward leg cut on the fourth count, it *joins* the left leg and both are swung around and over the left pommel into a rear support.

This is called a half double leg circle forward. You can do the other half by cutting your right leg forward on the second count, joining it to your left leg, and swinging both legs back and over the left pommel into a front support. This is a half double leg circle rearward.

If you've been wondering whether there's such a thing as a full double leg circle, you're absolutely right—there is. In fact the rules say that in all side horse routines, "double leg circles must predominate."

Now you'd think that doing a full double leg circle would be a simple matter of joining the two half leg circles you've already learned. And basically, it is. However, although a complete double leg circle isn't much more difficult physically, it is far more challenging than it at first appears.

The problem is that when the rules stipulate double leg circles, they don't mean simply doing the stunt at several places in your routine. What are called for are *continuous* double leg circles in which you move faster and raise your body further above the horse than when doing a half double leg circle.

This demands a great deal of coordination and often requires a considerable amount of time and practice to master. Consequently, while they are learning to do a double leg circle, most gymnasts use single leg cuts and half double leg circles in their routines instead.

Flank Mount and Flank Dismount

These two stunts get their names from the fact that your side or flank is nearest to the horse as you perform them. To do the flank mount, grasp both pommels and swing both legs up and over to the right (or left), cutting through your right (or left) hand. You'll finish in a rear support.

The flank dismount is done from a front support. From this position execute a half forward leg circle to the right (or left). Only do it a little faster than normal so that you leave the horse and land on the other side. Once released, your right arm should be pointed out to the side. Your left hand stays on the pommel as you land facing to the left. (Practice the flank mount and dismount to both sides.)

Flank mount and dismount: From this position you can either go into a rear support or continue forward and dismount.

Using the Whole Horse

All three parts of the horse must be used in a routine. So now that you know how to do some stunts, practice them at both ends of the horse. This means you'll grasp a pommel with one hand and place your other hand on the end of the horse. Then you perform a stunt just as if you were using the two pommels.

Working on either end of the horse will be a little more difficult than before. Both arms must be straight, so you'll be in a tilted position with one shoulder higher than the other. That changes your weight distribution and forces you to push "uphill" when shifting weight onto the hand holding the pommel. But practicing on both ends of the horse also gives you a more complete workout and better muscle development than working on just the center section.

Be sure to practice all of the stunts you've learned so far on both ends of the horse.

Basics of the Scissors

Every side horse routine must include scissors stunts. So let's start by grasping the left pommel with the right hand and placing the left hand on the end of the horse. Swing up and sit on the horse as if you were riding behind the saddle. Both hands should be on the pommel and you should be facing right.

Now, lean forward onto your wrists and lift yourself up as you swing your legs back behind you. When your legs have risen above the horse, scissor them so that they exchange positions. Your body will do a half twist to the left as your left leg moves up and over and your right leg comes down and under. As you scissor your legs, let go with your left hand and whip it over to regrasp the pommel on the other side of your right hand. As you sit down in your new position, release and regrasp the right hand.

The secret to this stunt is to keep your legs absolutely straight, toes pointed. It's not only good form, but it makes the scissors easier and keeps you from banging your knees on the horse.

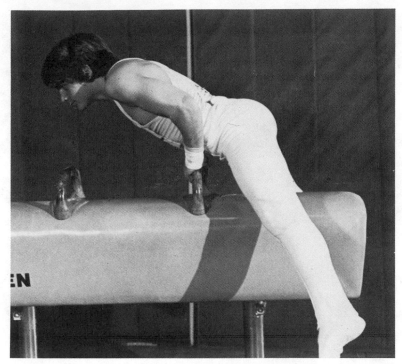

a. Begin from this position and lean forward onto the pommel.

THE BASICS OF THE SCISSORS

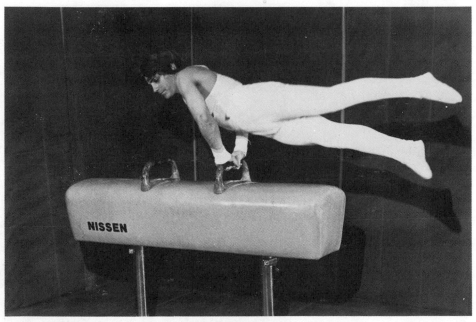

b. Swing your legs up high enough to clear the horse.

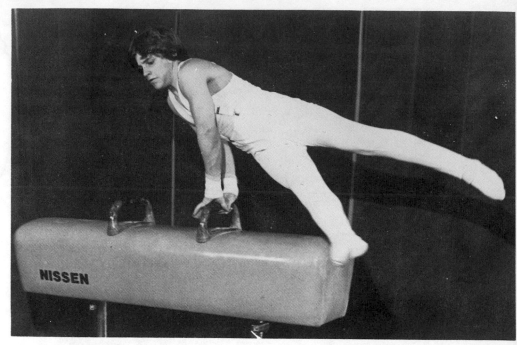

c. Then scissor them so that they exchange positions. The left leg moves up and over as the right leg comes down and under for a backward scissors.

d. The scissors motion causes your body to twist to the left, and you finish in this position.

Backward Scissors and Forward Scissors

With your right hand on the left pommel and your left hand on the end of the horse, do a left leg cut mount to a straddle support. You'll be facing forward and supporting your weight on your hands.

Start both legs swinging to the right and left at the same time. Shifting your weight from arm to arm in a rocking motion will help. On one of your swings to the left, try to get your legs up high enough to clear the horse. You'll have to lean hard to the right and release your left hand.

When your legs have cleared, scissor them so that the left leg goes back as the right leg goes forward. Swing back down again into a straddle, replacing your left hand on the end of the horse. Your right leg will now be in front and your left leg in the rear.

This is called a backward scissors because the top leg (your left leg) moves back. A forward scissors is done in exactly the same way, except that the top leg moves forward. Practice a forward scissors by getting your legs swinging again and then bringing your left leg forward as your right moves back. Then practice both kinds of scissors on the right end of the horse where the right leg will be on top.

Scissors in Series

Now try doing scissors while at the center of the horse. Do a single leg cut mount to a straddle support with a hand on each pommel and your right leg in front. Experiment with swinging your legs from left to right at the same time. Be sure to keep your hips between both arms as you're doing this so that both legs cross the horse at the same angle.

As you swing, try to lean so far to the left that you can release your right hand. Then lean to the right and release your left hand. Swing with the right leg in front for a while then take a rest and try it with the left leg in front.

As you swing, work on increasing the distance your legs move to either side. Gradually try to get them up above the horse. Then, once you're confident that you have enough time and clearance, do a forward scissors. Then swing again and do a backward scissors.

Try to develop a rhythm. When you really get going, try to mix the scissors up: forward scissors on the right, forward scissors on the left, backward scissors on the left, backward scissors on the right, and so forth.

Single Leg Travel

This stunt is used to move from one end of the horse to the other. Begin with a single leg cut mount to a straddle support in the center of the horse. Then do one series of rhythmical leg cuts, stopping in the front support position at the end of count four.

Next, cut your right leg forward. Follow by bringing your left leg forward as well, but *do not* release your left hand. You will end up with both legs forward and straddling your left arm. Most of your weight will be over the left pommel, but your right hand will still be on the right pommel.

Continue the stunt by bringing your right hand over and grasping the left pommel. At this point, swing your right leg to the rear just as you would for a leg cut. Then swing your left leg to the rear while simultaneously releasing your left hand and moving it to the left end of the horse. You will now be in a front support, having traveled from the center of the horse to its left end.

SINGLE LEG TRAVEL FROM THE END TO THE CENTER

a. Begin by standing at the left end of the horse and doing a left leg cut forward.

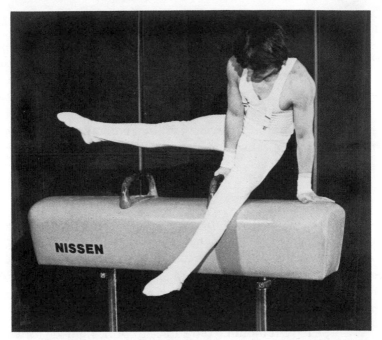

b. Cut your right leg forward and. . .

c. grasp the left pommel with both hands. Cut your left leg
   back and follow with your right. Grasp the right pommel
   with your right hand, and you'll be in a front support in
   the center of the horse.

As with leg cuts in series, the key to this stunt is to do it in "swing" time. Use one leg to knock the other leg back as in the leg cuts and try to develop that same 1-2-3-4 rhythm. This will make the single leg travel much easier than relying on sheer muscle power.

Be sure to practice this stunt traveling from center to right. And then try starting at one end, traveling to the center, and then traveling from the center to the other end.

Suggested Side Horse Routine

Once you've mastered the stunts in this chapter, you might want to try this beginning routine. Side horse stunts can be linked in an endless variety of ways, so look on the following routine as just one suggestion. After a while, you'll enjoy rearranging the stunts into an order of your own. As always, strive for smoothness and a feeling of one stunt flowing into the next.

1. Single leg cut mount to straddle support, right leg forward, on the right end of the horse.
2. Left leg cut forward.
3. Right leg cut rearward.
4. Left leg cut rearward. You'll now be in a front support.
5. Right leg cut forward.
6. Left leg cut forward, but do not release left hand. This begins the straddle travel stunt.
7. Right leg cut rearward as right hand joins left on pommel.
8. Left leg cut rearward as you place left hand on far pommel. You will now be in the center of the horse.
9. Right leg cut forward.
10. Left leg cut forward.
11. Right leg cut rearward.
12. Left leg cut rearward.
13. Both legs cut forward under right hand for a half double leg circle.
14. Left leg cut rearward.
15. Right leg cut rearward.
16. Left leg cut forward.
17. Forward scissors (Swing body up to the right side and release right hand. Right leg will end up in forward position.)

18. Left leg cut forward.

19. Right leg cut rearward.

20. Rearward scissors under left hand (Swing up to left side and release left hand. Right leg will end up in forward position.)

21. Right leg cut backward.

22. Left leg cut forward.

23. Forward scissors under the right hand.

24. Left leg cut forward, but left hand does not release. Begins straddle travel stunt.

25. Right leg cut rearward as right hand moves to left pommel.

26. Left leg cut rearward as left hand moves to end of horse. You will be in a front support at the left end of the horse.

27. Right leg cut forward.

28. Left leg cut forward.

29. Right leg cut rearward.

30. Left leg cut rearward.

31. Both legs cut forward under right hand to a flank dismount, landing facing to the left with left hand on end of the horse.

10
Competition and Careers

Now that you're on your way toward becoming an accomplished gymnast, let's take a look at the sport's competitive structure and organization.

At the international level the sport is governed by the Federation of International Gymnastics (F.I.G.). Based in Switzerland, the F.I.G. is a nonprofit organization that sets the rules for and helps to organize the Olympic Games, the World Championship, the European Cup, the Pan American Games, the International Student Championships, and most other contests between two or more nations.

The F.I.G. itself is made up of representatives from each country in the world that has an established gymnastics program. And it is more or less looked to as *the* authority on the sport. Other organizations, for example, usually adopt the official F.I.G. rules *in toto* or use them as the basis for their own rules.

The F.I.G. recognizes one national body in each country as its representative, and in America that organization is the United States Gymnastics Federation (U.S.G.F.). Based in Tucson, Arizona (P.O. Box 4699, ZIP: 85817), the U.S.G.F. has a number of functions. In addition to publishing a newsletter and a variety of other information on the sport, the U.S.G.F. also organizes exhibitions and national competition. A nonprofit organization, the U.S.G.F. does not charge a membership fee to competing gymnasts. It derives most of its income from the sale of its publications, exhibitions, and most important of all, from corporate grants and contributions.

The private sector, in fact, is absolutely essential to the health and success of American gymnastics. In many countries, gymnastics and other Olympic sports are funded primarily by the government or by quasi-governmental agencies. But in the United States this is not the case. Here we rely upon the contributions of private individuals and corporations, and many have enthusiastically responded with their support. AMF's American Athletic Equipment Division, for example, donates about $25,000 a year to the U.S.G.F. and often supplies equipment free of charge for many of the Federation's meets. Another company, the Dial Soap Division of Armour-Dial, Inc., has donated $1.2 million to cover U.S.G.F. operating expenses over a three-year period.

Such generosity has strengthened the sport considerably and helped to make possible the kind of training needed to produce world class gymnasts. A key element of that training is the U.S.G.F.'s age-level development program. This program provides a framework for gymnastics instruction and competitions geared to the athlete's age and level of ability. During the 1970s, the program has grown with the rising popularity of gymnastics and has already produced some outstanding competitors.

Many other organizations are also involved with gymnastics. The National Collegiate Athletic Association (N.C.A.A.), for example, has its own tournament structure and its own qualification procedures for individuals and teams competing for the National College Championship. The Amateur Athletic Union (A.A.U.) sponsors competitions. And classes and tournaments are offered by Y.M.C.A.'s, American Sokol organizations, the American Turners (Turnverein), state high school athletic organizations, and the many independent gymnastics clubs throughout the country. Most of these groups have their own tournament and competitive structures and championships.

How Olympic Teams are Chosen

All of these opportunities for competition allow gymnasts to hone their skills and perfect their routines, many with the possible aim of being selected for the U.S. Olympic team. Each year the U.S.G.F. holds its Championship of the U.S.A. competition. This is the major open meet in the sport and is the competition upon which a gymnast's national ranking is based.

However, in Olympic years and whenever a team must be selected for World Championship competition, the U.S.G.F. holds a special meet. Separate from the Championship of the U.S.A., this meet is held specifically for choosing an international team. A team consists of six gymnasts plus an alternate, and it's made up of the seven gymnasts who score highest in all-around (all event) competition.

Olympic Competition

The rules and procedures for Olympic and international meets are complex, and they may differ from those you'll encounter in other competitions. But here's the general way things work. In the first phase, everyone at the meet performs a compulsory routine in each event. The compulsories have been agreed upon beforehand and, by making everyone do the same stunts in the same order, are designed to provide a common basis for comparing the performance of each competitor.

In the second phase, everyone again performs in each event. But this time each gymnast presents an optional routine of his own creation. Here's where you can really show your stuff. Creativity, daring, originality, and overall effect are all considered in judging an optional routine.

At this point, each gymnast's scores from the first two phases are added together. The highest possible score in each event is 10.0, and since there are six events, a perfect score for a single phase is 60. Obviously a perfect score for both phases would be 120. Team scores are also tabulated using the top five individual scores for each event. Thus, 600 points is the highest possible team score.

After the top three teams have been announced, the thirty-six gymnasts with the highest all-around scores are invited to compete for the All-Around Championship. In this phase, the finalists perform another optional routine for each event. An individual's scores are then added to fifty percent of the total of his scores in the first two phases to determine the top three All-Around Champions.

Finally, there is the individual event competition. Performers are selected on the basis of their event scores in the first two phases, with the top eight gymnasts in each case being invited to compete for the championship of the event.

What It Takes

You don't have to be young to be an Olympic gymnast. In fact, while it isn't common, there have been some who didn't begin training until they were twenty-two or twenty-three. There have even been Olympic medal winners who are in their late thirties and early forties. At the other end of the scale, thanks to the U.S.G.F. age-level program, some boys have started at eight or nine and developed into world class gymnasts by the time they were seventeen. One member of the 1978 U.S. International Team, for example, was a senior in high school and another was a college freshman.

So age isn't all that important. What *is* important is a lot of hard work and dedication. The level of perfection required is so high that most prospective Olympians must train at least five and often six days a week. And with good reason. The time between the moment you do your first double leg circle on the horse, for example, and the day you can do it to Olympic perfection is not measured in weeks or months. It's measured in years. And that's only one stunt on one piece of apparatus.

A prospective Olympian must not only be willing to spend fifteen to twenty-five hours a week in the gym, he must also pay special attention to controlling his weight, to always getting enough sleep—in general, to taking superb care of his body. At the same time, he may also have to keep up with his schoolwork or work at a job to support himself.

All of this, as you can imagine, requires an awesome amount of motivation. But all Olympic gymnasts have it. They all have an overwhelming desire to be excellent and approach their work with the same single-minded dedication found in the true artist. Which is logical, because that's exactly what they are.

Yet while the work may be long and hard, the rewards are great. Few experiences in life can compare with competing in the Olympics and even fewer with being awarded an Olympic medal. But whether or not a gymnast earns a medal or even makes the Olympic team, he still wins. For at its heart, gymnastics is still an individual sport, and the satisfaction of knowing you gave your utmost—that you worked and worked until you were the best you could be—is the greatest experience of all.

Competing in a Meet

Gymnastics meets are one of the joys of the sport, for they give you a chance to show off all you've learned as you match your skills and stunts with your competitors. Yet since a gymnast's main competitor is really himself, there's a lot less of the competitive rivalry and possible bad feeling that sometimes characterizes other sports. As a result, a gymnastics tournament is often a good place to meet and make friends with other gymnasts.

There are two major types of gymnastics competition. There's the dual, triangular, quadrangular, or other meet in which two, three, four, or more teams compete. And there is the open meet in which gymnasts compete as individuals. Some organizations charge entry fees ranging from two dollars to about twelve dollars for open competition, and each group runs its meets a little differently. However, most use the same general procedures.

Obviously you or, if it's a team meet, your coach should make certain of the date, location, and time of the meet and see that the entry form is filled out and sent in on time. And, of course, you should be sure that your gymnastic pants, shirt, white socks, and gym slippers are clean and ready to wear. (A warm-up jacket or sweat shirt to keep your body temperature up while waiting to perform is also a good idea.)

There are some other things that you should take along as well. Most experienced gymnasts have a kit that they take with them to every meet. The kit contains all kinds of things and helps them be prepared for just about any emergency.

So right from the start you should probably get yourself a gym bag that you can stock with everything you'll need. Here's what you should have:

1. Palm guards, if you use them—for work on the high bar
2. A needle and thread—to mend rips in your pants or sew suspender buttons back on
3. Safety pins—for quick repairs when you don't have time to use a needle and thread

4. Athletic (adhesive) tape—for wrists, to cover blisters or tears, to mark your starting spot for the vault, to hold part of your uniform together in a pinch

5. One block of chalk in its wrapper—in case the meet runs out of chalk or uses a type you don't like

6. Emery paper—for smoothing the high bar and removing caked chalk left by previous performers

7. Extra fine sandpaper—for smoothing the parallel bars and pommels on the horse when necessary

8. Tape measure—for measuring your approach run for the vault

9. Towel, soap, and shower gear—these things are not usually supplied at a meet

10. Combination padlock—to put on gym lockers to protect your clothes and valuables

What to Do at an Open Meet

At team meets your coach will take care of most of the details. But at an open meet you're on your own. So the first thing to do is to find the registration desk and check in. You'll probably be assigned a competitor number and be given a printed order of warm-up and competition; or a sheet will be posted on a wall nearby.

Try to plan your warm-up so that you practice the events requiring equipment adjustments first. Check out the parallel bars, for instance, to see how they work and how they should be set for your routine. Try to get this done early, before everybody wants to warm up. As the meet's starting time gets closer, all the gymnasts who haven't warmed up will probably waste a lot of their time adjusting the equipment. Of course, if you're assigned a warm-up time for each event, you'll have to follow the prescribed order. But try to get your setting first so you'll know just what to do when your time comes.

Incidentally, it's a good idea to ask the person in front of you or behind you if they'd give you a hand adjusting the apparatus in exchange for your helping them. This will save you both a lot of time, and it's a good opportunity to meet your fellow gymnasts.

Your main goal in the warm-up is not so much to loosen your muscles and warm up your body as it is to familiarize yourself with the equipment and your surroundings. You're going to be performing in a different environment than you're used to. So if the sun is going to be in your eyes or if the apparatus doesn't feel quite the same as the equipment you've been practicing on, you will want to get used to it before the meet begins. You'll do your actual physical warm-up just before each event.

At the proper time the meet director will announce the end of the warm-up period. When that happens, resist the temptation to take one more swing on the apparatus. *Everyone* would like just one more swing, but if they all tried for it, there'd be chaos. By making a habit of obeying the director, you'll be doing your part to help the meet run smoothly.

There will probably be a special area set aside on the floor for competitors to sit while waiting their turns at each event. There should also be a place to do physical warm-ups—either a mat or in some cases a separate set of apparatus. As you await your turn you'll probably want to watch the other competitors perform. This is a lot of fun and a good opportunity to learn.

But whatever you do, don't let yourself get psyched out by what you see. Don't let somebody else's performance influence your opinion of your own routine.

You may, for example, see someone do a routine that's three times as difficult as yours and thus capable of scoring more points. But don't let it bother you. That's the level of gymnastics *he's* at. All you should be concerned with is doing the best possible job on the level *you're* at. There's nothing you can do to quickly learn an extra double back somersault and add it to your routine. If the other guy has one, he's got it, and there's nothing you can do about it today.

The same thing applies to the warm-up period. Don't let what you see there influence you at all. What you see in the warm-ups may not be what you see in competition. In fact, there are a lot of gymnasts who win the warm-up but lose the meet.

Taking Your Position

As your assigned time for performing in an event gets closer, go to the warm-up area and run through your stretching and flexibility exercises. By the time the person immediately preceding you in the competitive order is doing his routine, you should have your warm-up clothes off and be chalked up and ready to go.

Walk over near the event area so you'll be ready to trot out to adjust the apparatus (if necessary) as soon as the performing gymnast gets his applause and leaves. After you've made your adjustments, go back, put on a last bit of chalk, and stand near the apparatus. For the vault, the place to wait is at the end of the runway near your starting position.

The head judge will have been indicated to you at the beginning of the meet, and you should now face him. When he looks up at you, he'll give you the signal to start. Raise a hand to acknowledge the signal and walk to the apparatus to begin your routine. You'll undoubtedly be eager to get going, but do not walk to the apparatus until the judge gives you his signal.

Scoring

Normally there are either two or four judges at each event. Events are scored from 0 to 10.0 in a deductive way. A competitor begins with a perfect 10.0 but loses fractions of points for mistakes made along the way. However, the rules also provide for awarding bonus points based on risk, originality, and virtuosity. If there are two judges, their scores are averaged to produce a final result. If there are four judges, the highest and the lowest scores are tossed out and the two remaining scores are averaged.

Scoring procedures differ from one organization to another, so you should make a point of finding out how things are done at a meet before entering. Some meets award ribbons and some, medals. And as in any sport, there are sometimes ties.

Whenever there is a tie, a coin toss usually determines who gets to take the trophy home and who must wait for a duplicate to be mailed out later. If you are ever the one who must wait, it might be a good idea to get the name and address of the meet director in case the prize doesn't arrive when it should.

Careers in Gymnastics

Gymnastics can be habit-forming. But even though you will eventually stop competing, there's no reason why you can't still pursue your interest in the field. In addition to continuing to work out, you may even want to begin a career that's directly or indirectly connected with the sport. If that's the case, you're really in luck. With gymnastics growing all the time, there are lots of opportunities. Here are only some of the things you might consider.

Exhibition Gymnastics

You could prepare a program to be presented at high school assemblies. This might be particularly appealing to someone with an outgoing personality who might enjoy demonstrating his skills and giving a little talk on gymnastics. The job would involve a lot of traveling, but some people enjoy living on the move.

Coaching and Teaching

This is a traditional career path for former athletes, but in gymnastics it's recently become hotter than ever. The fact is, gymnastics is expanding so fast that the demand for coaches has soared in the past few years. There just aren't enough to fill all the jobs that are available at schools, colleges, and service organizations.

Good teachers, especially for the beginning and advanced levels, are also in demand. This is particularly true for the growing number of private gymnastics clubs. Teaching is a skill that's quite different from performing. People who are capable of not only executing a stunt but also showing others how to do it are in extremely short supply.

You have to be a gymnast for this job, but a background in education is far more important than the number of medals you've won in competition. The need is so great that we've recently founded this country's first gymnastics academy with a curriculum aimed at teaching gymnasts how to teach gymnastics. Our aim is to turn out skilled, professional gymnastics instructors capable of organizing and administering a complete gymnastics program.

Research

For the technically minded, there are careers in biomechanics, kinesiology (the study of anatomy as it relates to movement), and physiology. Several colleges, institutions, and sports medicine centers conduct research programs in these and related fields, and gymnastics is basic to all of them.

Sales

If you like selling, there are careers in the sports equipment field that are directly related to gymnastics. As a present or former gymnast you'll know all about the apparatus and how to best satisfy a customer's equipment needs. And you may even have made some friends during your competitive years who would be excellent sales contacts.

Design

Every piece of apparatus you've ever used was designed by someone. And as a former gymnast, you'll have an invaluable insight into what equipment should be like. You may even have some ideas on how a piece of apparatus could be improved or on some modification that would make it easier to use.

School or Camp Operation

If you have an entrepreneurial flair and a good head for business, you might want to open your own gymnastics school or summer camp. This is currently the fastest growing area in gymnastics. And while it's a lot of hard work, you're your own boss and head of your own business.

Being a counselor/instructor at a gymnastics summer camp is a good way to get started. It doesn't pay a lot, but it gives you an idea of what teaching and managing are like. And it's one of the few summer jobs where you can train and get paid for it.

As we said earlier, these are only a few of the avenues that are open to you when you finish competing. As you get into things, you'll discover many more. And you'll see how your interest in gymnastics can give you not only a sport you'll enjoy the rest of your life, but a challenging career opportunity as well.

ABOUT THE AUTHOR----

Doug Alt has been involved with gymnastics, either as a competitor or as an instructor, nearly all of his life. A former gymnastics coach for Princeton University and one of fourteen directors of the U.S. Gymnastics Federation, Doug began his career as a freshman in high school at a time when Americans were just beginning to discover the sport. As a sophomore, he became one of the first members of his school's team and contributed to several undefeated seasons.

Later, at Springfield College in Springfield, Massachusetts, Doug earned a degree in physical education and continued his gymnastics training. In his senior year, he qualified for the N.C.A.A. National Championships on the horizontal bar and was ranked seventh in the nation in all-around competition at the 1965 U.S. Gymnastics Federation Championships, the forerunner of today's Championship of the U.S.A.

After college, Doug taught physical education in elementary school while earning extra money playing keyboards and bass for a rock band. A two-year hitch in the army followed, during which Doug was stationed in Eschborn, a small town just outside of Frankfurt, West Germany. Three days after his arrival, he discovered a gymnastics club within walking distance of the base and, although he spoke no German, was enthusiastically invited to join. Later that year, Eschborn celebrated its one thousand two hundredth birthday, and to commemorate the event, a biannual all-sports competition was established. Doug and his fellow gymnastics club members entered and when the competition was over, the ancient town of Eschborn crowned its first champion—Joseph Douglas Alt from Morganville, New Jersey.

Following his army service, Doug returned home and soon opened a gymnastics school in a small barn on a farm near Shrewsbury, New Jersey. The school quickly outgrew its modest quarters and had to be moved into town. There are now four Alt's Gymnastics Schools, with a total of nearly three thousand students of all age and ability levels. A number of Doug's students have reached the national level in either age group or open competition, and in 1978 one of them qualified for a place in the U.S.G.F. National Development Program, the official training program for the U.S. Olympic team.

Index